U-1009 – *the first U-boat to enter Loch Eriboll – before formal arrest. She is still flying the tattered black flag of surrender. At the time it was claimed that* U-249 *was the first U-boat to enter a British port, at Weymouth. But* U-1009 *surrendered to the 21st Escort Group and entered Loch Eriboll in the early morning of 10 May 1945. HMS* Byron *can be seen in the background (Imperial War Museum)*

The Grey Wolves of Eriboll

David M. Hird

Whittles Publishing

Published by
Whittles Publishing,
Dunbeath,
Caithness KW6 6EY,
Scotland, UK

www.whittlespublishing.com

© 2010 David M. Hird

ISBN 978-1904445-32-6

Printed by

Bell & Bain Ltd., Glasgow

For Iris and Donnie Mackay, native-born Durnessian and Eribollsider respectively,
with grateful affection after many years true friendship

Contents

MAP SHOWING POSITIONS OF
SURRENDERING U-BOATS
9–20 MAY 1945

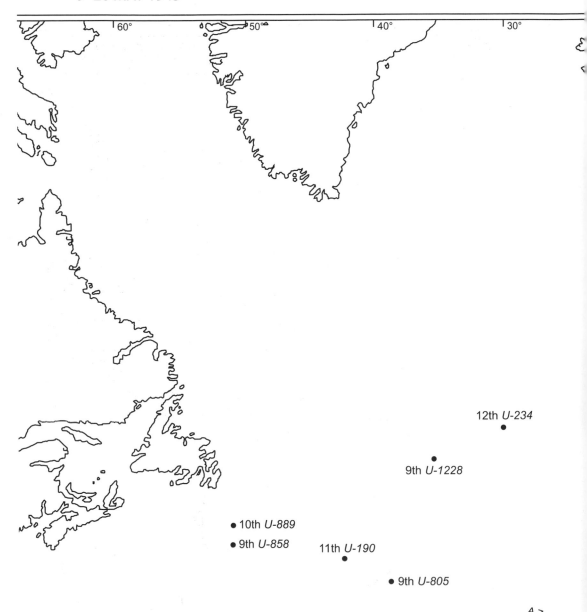

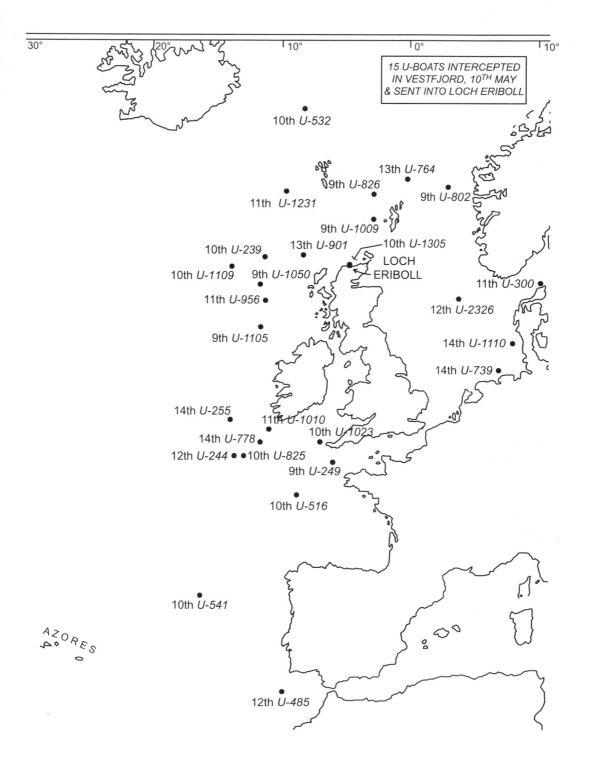

30° 20° 10° 0° 10°

15 U-BOATS INTERCEPTED
IN VESTFJORD, 10TH MAY
& SENT INTO LOCH ERIBOLL

10th *U-532*

13th *U-764*
9th *U-826*
11th *U-1231*
9th *U-802*
9th *U-1009*
10th *U-239*
13th *U-901*
10th *U-1305*
10th *U-1109* 9th *U-1050*
LOCH ERIBOLL
11th *U-956*
11th *U-300*
12th *U-2326*
9th *U-1105*
14th *U-1110*
14th *U-739*
14th *U-255*
11th *U-1010*
10th *U-1023*
14th *U-778*
12th *U-244* 10th *U-825*
9th *U-249*
10th *U-516*
10th *U-541*

AZORES

12th *U-485*

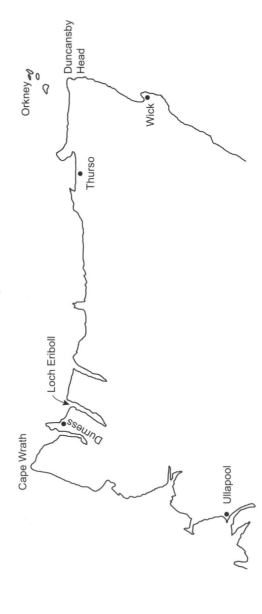

THE FAR NORTH OF SCOTLAND

N

Shetland

Orkney

Duncansby
Head

Wick

Thurso

Loch Eriboll

Durness

Cape Wrath

Ullapool

Loch Alsh

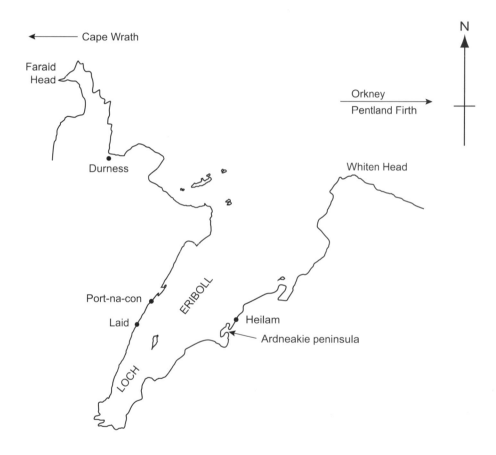

Cape Wrath

Faraid
Head

N

Orkney
Pentland Firth

Durness

Whiten Head

Port-na-con

ERIBOLL

Laid

Heilam

Ardneakie peninsula

LOCH

LOCH ERIBOLL AND ENVIRONS

Loch Eriboll, eastern shore. This part of Loch Eriboll, between the distinctive twin-crescent Ard Neackie peninsula and Port-na-con on the western shore, was where the British and Canadian frigates of the 21st and 9th Escort Groups moored with their Kriegsmarine captives. Armaments, explosives and torpedo parts were thrown into the loch here (Author's collection)

Loch Eriboll, western shore. The tiny settlement of Port-na-con with its pier. The timber extension in this pre-war photograph is long gone. The U-boats remained here only a matter of hours, in most cases, before escort to Loch Alsh and then onwards to Loch Ryan or Lough Foyle, Northern Ireland (Author's collection)

Acknowledgements

Without the involvement of those who were present in Loch Eriboll in those heady days at the close of the Second World War this book would not have appeared in the form that it has, and I am sincerely grateful to those who, in response to my many letters and messages, provided detailed memories of their experiences.

Alan Hope was my first significant contact. His personal reminiscences combined with the account on which he collaborated with his late Royal Navy colleague John Whithouse, recalling the part played by HMS *Byron* of the 21st Escort Group in the first formal arrests in Loch Eriboll, provided the impetus from which my determination to fully research those events sprang. The very detailed diary kept by his shipmate Cliff Greenwood provides a primary account of the U-boat surrenders. It is so providential that a copy survived to be deposited in the Imperial War Museum archives; I feel doubly fortunate that I have been able to include extracts from it via the HMS *Byron* newsletter No. 10, which directly describes the surrenders. That Cliff Greenwood, prior to his wartime service, was a newspaper journalist surely makes his recorded impressions so much more powerful.

Later in my researches I made contact with former crew members of HMCS *Nene*, one of the Canadian frigates of the 9th Escort Group tasked with responsibility for the safe escort of a flotilla of fifteen U-boats intercepted off the Norwegian coast to Loch Eriboll in May 1945, the largest group U-boat surrender throughout the war years. Ken Riley, Ron Graham, Howard Elliott and Sam Forsythe, now contentedly retired in Canada, were each most helpful. They all willingly provided information from their memories extending back sixty-five years, and again I am most grateful that I have been able to include their contributions. I was able to contact them through the good offices of Dan Delong (son of the late Don Delong, also a *Nene* shipmate) who remains very active in preserving memories of the frigate and her crew. (See http://timetraces.ca/nene)

Pat Stevens, site webmaster of the Destroyer Escort Sailors Association (www.desausa. org) kindly gave permission for me to print the article entitled 'The Forgotten Operation', written in 2004 by Pat Godwin, crew member of HMS *Fitzroy* also of the 21st Escort Group. The website is dedicated to preserving the memory of the lend-lease American-built frigates ('Destroyer Escorts' in American parlance) which were so vital to the British in combating the U-boat threat over the entire north Atlantic. Once the enemy were defeated then these same vessels were significantly employed in the immediate post-war operations in both British and foreign waters.

Ian Lindsey and Percy Blunden each responded to an appeal kindly printed in the West *Highland Free Press* on my behalf. Their recollections add further colour to the wider story of the surrenders and their aftermath. Walter and John Clarke and Michael Mather were the very few surviving Durness and Loch Eriboll locals with personal memories of the immediate post-war days whom I was able to contact. They each willingly gave their time and allowed me to record their memories.

I must record my appreciation to two individuals who were instrumental in supporting me in my researches and who provided much-needed corroborative documentary data when I became almost submerged (there really is no way of avoiding the pun) in the vast amount of detail generated by the project. Vidar Teigen is a Norwegian U-boat enthusiast (and a former submariner) with a consuming interest in U-boat matters in general and *U-992* in particular. He possesses a wide knowledge of most of the intricacies of what is really a very specialised subject. He always found time to provide easily digestible explanations to my questions; his support was invaluable. And Martin Pegg is a meticulous naval researcher. He is insistent upon searching out original source documentation and is thoroughly immersed in the entire subject of the surrender of the Kriegsmarine in 1945. He has a vast knowledge of the subject and I am sure that the result of his researches, when published, will form a very important asset to the corpus of knowledge currently in the public domain.

Early in my researches I made contact with the Imperial War Museum with a view to obtaining copies of any remaining photographs of the Loch Eriboll receptions. The volume of available material quite surprised me. Obviously the entire official Admiralty photographic record compiled at the time, both from surface ships and aircraft accompanying surrendering U-boats, survived into modern times and it is surely to the advantage of all that it was carefully catalogued, itemised and preserved in the IWM archives. I wish to place on record my appreciation of the help Ian Proctor and Simon Offord provided in identifying all of the relevant images.

The Ministry of Defence Naval Historical Branch in Portsmouth were similarly most helpful in furnishing corroborations of the results of my research. I am particularly grateful for the assistance and interest shown by WO1 Harry McLoughlin in that regard. The National Archives of Canada also hold a fund of information on the part played in the Second World War by Canadian personnel and warships. Their staff were eager to assist in identifying relevant photographs and contemporary records, and I wish to record my sincere gratitude for their interest and support.

The archives of *The Scotsman* newspaper proved invaluable in my efforts to access the officially sanctioned press reports of the day, and I am happy once again to record my thanks for their approval of my including the relevant extracts, without which there would be no corresponding narrative. No further interpretative comment is necessary. The newspaper reports of the day say all that need be said. I naturally trawled through back copies of the local Sutherland newspaper – *The Northern Times*, or 'The Raggie' – searching for some comment, however brief, reflecting the internationally important events taking place in our very far north-western backwater. But there was absolutely nothing. I must record my thanks to Nicky

Blackburn and Shirley MacLean of Brora Library for helping me to prove the negative so comprehensively, never a simple task at the best of times. Towards the end of the project the editor of *The Northern Times* kindly printed my letter appealing for reminiscences, for which I am grateful.

I owe a considerable debt of gratitude to those publishers on whom I have relied within the text for permission to quote from their own publications. My primary source for the details and dates of the individual U-boat data given in chapter six was Peter Sharpe's *U-Boat Fact File*, originally published in 1998 by Midland Publishing. The book now falls within the purview of the Ian Allan organisation, and I am grateful to Nick Grant for allowing me to rely heavily on that source. As a comprehensive introduction to the whole U-boat sub-culture I can recommend no better work than Peter Sharpe's.

GC Books Ltd of Wigtown and Richard Holme, author of the book *Cairnryan: Military Port 1940–1996*, detailing the development of the military port at Cairnryan, readily agreed to my quoting from that source, for which I am extremely grateful. The need for the early wartime construction of secure port facilities on the west coast of Britain arose due to the proximity of our east coast parts to attacks by the Luftwaffe. Those same facilities provided the means by which the surrendered U-boats would eventually be destroyed.

Foulsham Publishing Ltd readily agreed to my quoting verbatim the extract from Lund and Ludlam's *Atlantic Jeopardy* relating the part played in the U-boat surrenders by the armed trawlers of Harry Tate's Navy. I gratefully acknowledge their approval here.

It cannot be denied that the Internet today provides an extremely effective research tool. But its resources must be treated with great circumspection, for there is a great deal of misinformation within the World Wide Web. Nothing can be taken at face value nor accepted as fact without detailed checking and positive verification. There are discussion forums covering every subject imaginable, and U-boats are no exception. But equally there is much opinion, supposition and theory presented as fact, which is very dangerous indeed. Enthusiasts, or even those sufficiently inspired by this book to delve deeper, would be well advised to seek verification from authoritative publications before accepting as fact anything proposed as so on the Internet. There is no real substitute for contemporary documentation compiled by eye-witnesses intent on setting out an accurate and unbiased record for posterity.

Those websites which I have found useful in providing a basic grounding in the vast sub-culture of the U-boat include www.uboataces.com under the overall supervision of David Oearn. David readily agreed to my using his graphics of the emblems and insignia displayed by most of the boats received into Loch Eriboll, and he further agreed to my using the article describing the trials of life in a U-boat on which my corresponding piece is based. I found www.dutchsubmarines.com particularly useful in determining the tortuous service life of one former Royal Netherlands Navy boat absorbed into the Kriegsmarine during the period under review which may have a Loch Eriboll connection. I am grateful for permission to use their collated facts in respect of that boat. Mention must also be made of www.uboat.net(*) and www.ubootwaffe.net, arguably the two leading websites in the subject. Each contains a wealth of information on all of the U-boats produced and operated by the Kriegsmarine, and each provides a lively discussion forum supported by enthusiastic members keen to impart knowledge (and opinion) without straying into controversy. Via the medium of the former(*) Ken Dunn quickly identified *U-968*, on the deck of which were photographed the three Canadian naval personnel principally involved in the boat's boarding and formal surrender.

My final acknowledgement must be towards Keith Whittles, my publisher, and his expert staff. As completion of my research project approached I became aware of the pressing need to find a competent publisher, preferably in the north of Scotland, able to recognise the local significance of the subject matter and willing to make a reasonably long-term commitment. I made my first tentative approach as long ago as February 2009. That same month he agreed in principle to accept the finished typescript in November 2009 with a view to publication in May of 2010. After minimal contact between us thereafter he brought the project to publication, on time, and I like to think that we all remain friends.

Two and a half years ago I knew nothing about either Loch Eriboll's silent secret or of the sinister engines of war brought there for ultimate destruction. I knew nothing of the heroes who received their adversaries in this broodingly magnificent place. In the intervening months I have expanded my knowledge of times long gone and of the young men brought together by the vicissitudes of global warfare. I have made sincere friends along the way, some of whom I have still not met, but nevertheless I do regard them all with genuine affection.

Without the commitment of combatants and the encouragement of enthusiasts, this story could not have been told.

Introduction

This work emerged by happy accident, as do all of life's small exquisite pleasures.

I had completed the text and final editing of *A Light in the Wilderness*, my study of the Cape Wrath peninsula at the very far north-western tip of the British mainland, and publication day approached with unstoppable inevitability. As a possible next research project I was actively considering a picture-based study of Sutherland's west and north coasts highlighting the changes that had been witnessed over the past, say, seventy-five years.

Preparatory work for that general overview brought Loch Eriboll into my sights. Today this is a wild, spectacular wilderness landscape on the far north coast of Sutherland, nowadays fully accessed by the A838 road as it meanders east–west between Durness and Tongue, alternately hugging the coastline or rising to cross convoluted bedrock unchanged since the dawn of time. But even as recently as the 1930s this road, largely unsurfaced and wholly single-track, would have presented something of an expedition to the few intrepid motorists able or willing to attempt it. Clearly the road has had to make allowances for the geography and geology hereabouts – highways go where they are permitted by the topography to go; they do not strike out arrow-straight for their next objective.

It gradually became apparent to me that Eriboll's brooding sea loch kept something of a secret close to itself, notwithstanding the fact that its long-time naval connections were proclaimed high on the valley side where the names of famous and not-so-famous British warships announce to the world their past presence. Firm details of the secret were difficult to tease from the vast amount of myth and obfuscation forming much of the Internet today, but there was just sufficient there to sustain my interest. And any event allegedly predicted by the Brahan Seer centuries ago must surely be worthy of investigation.

Eventually it became clear that although Loch Eriboll provided a deep-water anchorage for the capital ships of the British Navy during and after the First World War, the real story lay in the last acts of the 1939–45 conflict. Even today this is a supremely peaceful, awe-inspiring place, doubtless the source of wonderment to the very many thousands of visitors intent on making the journey 'across the top' of the British mainland.

Loch Eriboll made its own contribution to the peace of 1945 in a manner quite unforeseen by anyone other than the few naval planners managing the day-to-day conduct of the War. Whilst the happenings of May 1945 were never closely guarded state secrets kept strictly from public knowledge, there was little contemporary publicity nationally and none locally proclaiming the significant part Loch Eriboll played. There was just no mention in the local press of the time of Loch Eriboll and the internationally momentous events taking place there in that spring of 1945. Bare facts did filter out piecemeal (still recognisable today as heavily news-managed) into the national newspapers, but generally the events in Eriboll were overshadowed by the supremely significant nature of those incidents, and the accident of geography never assumed any importance in the public psyche. Whilst ordinary Britons were swept up in the delirium of the first heady days of peace, they cared little for and were allowed to know less of just where the moves of the War's endgame were being choreographed.

Tenacity and a consuming interest bordering on obsession eventually revealed the whole fascinating story of the part Loch Eriboll played in the surrender, arrest and ultimate demise of Germany's U-boat fleet, a force developed with the prime intention of starving the British Isles into submission and an aim which so nearly succeeded during the dark days of June 1940 to February 1941 and January to August 1942, *die glückliche Zeite* ('the happy times') for the U-boat wolfpacks ranging the Atlantic.

Loch Eriboll was designated as early as August 1944 as the principal reception location for operational U-boats at sea to the north of the British Isles at the time of the capitulation. Naval Intelligence assessments suggested that up to 160 U-boats might be at sea when the surrender came, though it was acknowledged that due to the many variables which could have a direct effect on matters, a reliable forecast might well be much smaller.

Representatives of the Allies and the German High Command drew up an order dated 7 May 1945 setting out the precise procedures for the surrender of German U-boats then at sea. All U-boats were required to surface and surrender to Allied forces as soon as practicable. In the seas around Scotland (the Western Approaches of the north Atlantic, and the North Sea between northern mainland Europe and the Scottish coast) U-boats were required to steam in open view towards Loch Eriboll. Specific navigation courses and channels were designated ('Blue' route and 'Red' route) along which surfaced vessels, prominently displaying a black or blue flag of surrender, were required to sail to await arrest, escort and impounding.

The first U-boat to surface and radio its position to the Allied forces was *U-1105*, at 0907 hours on Wednesday, 9 May when in the Atlantic west of Ireland. This vessel entered Loch Eriboll under escort on the following day and was the third one to arrive. The first surrendered U-boat to enter Loch Eriboll was *U-1009*, at 0700 on 10 May. The last U-boat to be escorted into Loch Eriboll, according to the official record, was *U-295* on 19 May, although a claim for that honour has been made naming *U-2529*, on 3 June.

Initially eighteen surrendered U-boats were escorted into Loch Eriboll by the 21st Escort Group between 10 and 18 May 1945. On 19 May frigates of the 9th (Canadian) Escort Group, which had been on convoy duty to Russia but which were detached when it became clear that a large group of surrendered boats was in their vicinity, brought in a further fifteen U-boats. All of these surrendered U-boats were boarded, disarmed and rendered safe in Loch Eriboll before being escorted to the more permanent holding locations at Loch Ryan on the west coast, or Ulster. A formal surrender ceremony took place at Lisahally, Lough Foyle, Northern Ireland.

Some sources are really quite adamant that a very few further U-boats arrested in Norwegian waters were escorted into Loch Eriboll at the end of May and the beginning of June 1945, after the departure of the 21st and 9th Escort Groups. However, no reception facilities remained at Loch Eriboll except a couple of Royal Navy Patrol Service armed trawlers ('Harry Tate's Navy') patrolling the waters between the Minch and the Pentland Firth, and surrendered vessels would therefore have to be taken immediately onwards to the west coast storage and impounding areas. I am prepared to accept that a very few escorted U-boats *could* have appeared briefly in Loch Eriboll around the beginning of June 1945 (though the official record is adamant that this was not so), just as I am sure that there are errors in the published histories claiming that many U-boats did so.

The official record shows that a certain total of thirty-three surrendered U-boats were escorted to temporary berths in the waters of Loch Eriboll during May 1945. Most stayed only a matter of hours, but there are additional candidates, and therefore the possible total has been quoted as nearer forty. Doubts persist and disputes continue as to the 'also-rans' and 'possibles', and I have identified these additional vessels separately in the body of the text so that errors of fact will not be perpetuated.

By far the majority of the surrendered U-boats became part of Operation Deadlight, an agreement between the governments of the Allied forces which provided for their permanent destruction. But there were exceptions. Some thirty captured U-boats were apportioned to the Allied navies under the Tripartite Naval Agreement of 3 November 1945, for evaluation, testing and research purposes, and they evaded the Operation Deadlight fate.

A handful of the Loch Eriboll U-boats became part of this select band. A further vessel enjoyed an even more unusual career. It started service in the navy of one invaded nation, was absorbed into the navy of the aggressor only to be returned to its originator after the end of hostilities. It survived in service until 1959, and was not dismantled until 1961. Just one Loch Eriboll U-boat remains accessible, by specially equipped sport divers, in the eastern United States. And one surface vessel at the centre of the Loch Eriboll events all those years ago remains on active service, very much in the public eye and an object of national reverence, today.

I do hope that what follows provides an enthralling story from a time when the world was very different. I trust also that the technical aspects of the story are not overwhelming. It is a difficult task to make the story move along and to hold the reader's interest when describing a technology the ultimate fate of which was to be consigned to the depths of the north Atlantic Ocean in the middle years of the last century.

In the last sixty-five years western Europe has changed virtually beyond recognition. National governments have put in place measures designed primarily to ensure that global conflicts are avoided before they are able again to disrupt international peace.

Yet, despite the large-scale events and manifestations of ill will preceding the end of the last global conflict, Loch Eriboll continues to rest in much the same peaceful serenity with which it has always, in the main, been associated.

David M. Hird
Dalchalm
Sutherland

THE SURRENDER ORDER OF THE GERMAN U-BOAT FLEET

The Act of Military Surrender to end the war in Europe was signed at Rheims, France at 0241 hours on 7 May 1945. Signatories were:

On behalf of the German High Command
JODL
In the presence of
On behalf of the Supreme Commander, Allied Expeditionary Force
W.B. SMITH
On behalf of the Soviet High Command
SOUSLOPAROV

F. SEVEZ
Major General, French Army (Witness)

The surrender instrument itself is an extensive document of thirty-nine sections with sub-sections and paragraphs extending over nine pages setting out every eventuality and condition affecting the nations of the signatory participants. Addenda referred specifically to provisions for the surrender of German naval forces, and particular emphasis was placed on the precise manner in which U-boats at sea would present themselves for surrender to British and Allied forces and at British ports. Loch Eriboll was selected as the principal surrender location for North Sea and Atlantic fleet vessels. Precise navigational routes were set out by which surrendering U-boats must approach that point.

The relevant addenda are set out below.

Annexure A

Surrender of German U-boat fleet
To all U-boats at sea:

(1) Carry out the following instructions forthwith which have been given by the Allied Representatives
    (a) Surface immediately and remain surfaced.
    (b) Report immediately in P/L your position in latitude and longitude and number of your U-boat to nearest British, US, Canadian or Soviet coast W/T station on 500 kc/s (600 metres) and to call sign GZZ 10 on one of the following high frequencies: 16845 – 12685 or 5970 kc/s.
    (c) Fly a large black or blue flag by day.
    (d) Burn navigation lights by night.
    (e) Jettison all ammunition, remove breach blocks from guns and render torpedoes safe by removing pistols. All mines are to be rendered safe.
    (f) Make all signals in P/L.
    (g) Follow strictly the instructions for proceeding to Allied ports from your present area given in immediately following message.
    (h) Observe strictly the orders of Allied Representatives to refrain from scuttling or in any way damaging your U-boat.

(2) These instructions will be repeated at two-hourly intervals until further notice.

Annexure B

To all U-boats at sea. Observe strictly the instructions already given to remain fully surfaced. Report your position, course and speed every 8 hours. Obey any instructions that may be given to you by any Allied authority.

(1) Area 'A'
    (a) Bound on West by meridian 026 degs West and South by parallel 043 degs North, in Barents Sea by meridian 020 degs East, in Baltic Approaches by line joining the Naze and Hantsholm but excludes Irish Sea between 051 degs thirty mins and 055 degs 00 mins North and English Channel between line of Lands End–Scilly Islands–Ushant and line of Dover–Calais.
    (b) Join one of following routes at nearest point and proceed along it to Loch Eriboll (058 degs 33 minutes North 004 degs 37 minutes West).

        Blue route: All positions North and West unless otherwise indicated

        049 degs 00 mins
        009 degs 00 mins
        053 degs 00 mins
        012 degs 00 mins

058 degs 00 mins

011 degs 00 mins

059 degs 00 mins

005 degs 30 mins

Thence to Loch Eriboll.

Red route:

053 degs 45 mins North

003 degs 00 mins East

059 degs 45 mins

001 degs 00 mins

059 degs 45 mins

003 degs 00 mins

Thence to Loch Eriboll.

    (c)   Arrive at Loch Eriboll between sunrise and 3 hours before sunset.

(2)   Area 'B'

    (a)   The Irish Sea between parallel of 051 degs 30 mins and 055 degs 00 mins North.

    (b)   Proceed Beaumaris Bay (053 degs 19 mins North 003 degs 58 mins West) to arrive between sunrise and 3 hours before sunset.

(3)   Area 'C'

    (a)   The English Channel between line of Lands End–Scilly Isles–Ushant and line of Dover–Calais.

    (b)   U-boats in area 'C' are to join one of the following routes at nearest point: Green route: position 'A' 049 degs 10 mins North 005 degs 40 mins West, position 'B' 050 degs 00 mins North 003 degs 00 mins West thence escorted to Weymouth. Orange route: position 'X' 050 degs 30 mins North 000 degs 50 mins East; position 'Y' 050 degs 10 mins North 001 degs 50 mins West thence escorted to Weymouth.

    (c)   Arrive at either 'B' or 'Y' between sunrise and 3 hours before sunset.

(4)   Area 'D'

    a.   Bound on West by lines joining The Naze and Hantsholm and on East by lines joining Lubeck and Trelleborg.

    b.   Proceed to Kiel.

(5)   Area 'E'

    a.   Mediterranean Approaches bound on North by 043 degs North on South by 026 degs North and on West by 026 degs West.

    b.   Proceed to a rendezvous in position 'A' 036 degs 00 mins North 011 degs 00 mins West and await escort reporting expected time of arrival in plain language to Admiralty Gibraltar on 500 kc/s.

    c.   Arrive in position 'A' between sunrise and noon GMT

(6)   Area 'F'

    a.   The North and South Atlantic West of 026 degs West.

    b.   Proceed to nearest of one of following points arriving between sunrise and 3 hours before sunset: 'W' 043 deg 30 mins North 070 degs 00 mins West approach from a point 15 miles due East; 'X' 038 degs 20 mins North 074 degs 25 mins West approach from a point 047 degs 18 mins North 051 degs 30 mins West on a course 270 degs; 'Z' 043 degs 31 mins North 065 degs 05 mins West approach from a point 042 degs 59 mins North 054 degs 28 mins West on a course 320 degs.

Undertaking given by
certain German emmissaries to
the Allied High Commands

It is agreed by the German emissaries undersigned that the following German officers will arrive at a place and time designated by the Supreme Commander, Allied Expeditionary Force, and the Soviet High Command prepared, with plenary powers, to execute formal ratification on behalf of the German High Command of this Act of Unconditional Surrender of the German armed forces.

- Chief of the High Command
- Commander-in-Chief of the Army
- Commander-in-Chief of the Navy
- Commander-in-Chief of the Air Force

SIGNED

JODL

Representing the German High Command

DATED 0241 hrs 7 May 1945
Rheims, France

Personal recollections (1)

The following accounts are reminiscences written by combatants present in Loch Eriboll at the time of the momentous events of the early summer of 1945. They were written by individuals who were there because they were obliged to be there – they were service personnel directly involved in the arrest, delivery and subsequent dispersal of the surrendered U-boats. The events made lasting impressions on those who witnessed them. These personal narratives were written, in the main, some sixty years after the events they describe. It is a measure of the significance of their importance in the lives of these ordinary people that the memories remain so clear after the passage of all those years.

Alan Hope, Petty Officer Radio Mechanic, Captain Class Frigate
HMS *Byron* (K.508), Loch Eriboll, May 1945

At the end of the war I was serving aboard HMS *Byron* (K.508) as part of the 21st Escort Group. I maintained contact with shipmates long after the end of the war and, as a member of the HMS *Byron* Association began, with others some years ago, to record the history of the ship from recollections written by other members.

We produced sixteen quarterly issues and the following extract from issue number ten covers the Loch Eriboll and U-boat surrender period.

HMS *Byron* Newsletter

No. 10. Autumn, 1994

1   NORTH ATLANTIC   29 April 1945–6 May 1945

During the evening of 29 April aircraft reported five U-boats on the surface about 100 miles away to the north-west, so we sailed from Lough Foyle, sadly without *Redmill*, and headed for their position. The weather, however, was atrocious and it took seven hours of hard pounding to arrive in the area. The aircraft was still there, but the U-boats weren't and the search was abandoned on 1 May. Instead, we supported a convoy to the vicinity of Oversay, and then escorted another for a couple of hundred miles westward into the Atlantic. By this time we were short of fuel and spent 5 and 6 May in Lisahally.

We sailed on 7 May, with the uncompleted High Tea barrier still in mind, but this now pointless errand was quickly aborted, and the Group sailed in company north to accept the surrender of the U-boats ordered to Loch Eriboll.

2   TO: ALL U BOATS   FROM: GRAND ADMIRAL DOENITZ

'You must now make the hardest sacrifice of all for your Fatherland by obeying the following instructions unconditionally. This casts no slur on your honour but will prevent serious consequences for your native land.

T.O.O.   081945Z.

The following instructions of the Allied representatives are to be complied with forthwith.

1. Henceforth to proceed on the surface only.
2. Report the ship's number and position in longitude and latitude in plain language to the nearest British, North American, Canadian or Russian shore wireless station on 600 m (500 k/cs) or on short-wave 16845 or 12685 or 5970 k/cs with call sign GZZ 110.
3. By day fly large black or blue flag.
4. At night show lights.
5. Throw all ammunition overboard, remove breech mechanism of guns and firing unit of torpedoes, secure mines.

6. W/T and signals traffic only in P/L.
7. Comply rigidly with all instructions given in a signal immediately following this for course and speed to Allied harbour.
8. The order given out by the Allies against scuttling or damaging of vessels is to be complied with. These instructions will be repeated till further notice at all calling-up times in accordance with *Distelschaltung* and also at two-hourly intervals.

3 LOCH ERIBOLL   8 May 1945 – 23 May 1945

VE Day, 8 May, was a day of bright sunshine and stiff breezes and we sailed north through the Minches with the Scottish coast to starboard and the islands of the Hebrides to port, both clearly visible and with the upper deck loudspeakers tuned to the BBC and the voice of Montgomery accepting the German surrender. We Spliced the Mainbrace – or rather I didn't, being Under Age. (I resented this, and said so, frequently. Alan, as it happens, was also UA. I reckon the Navy owes us both a tot) (JW).

There were just the five ships of 21EG at Loch Eriboll, together with the Motor Launch C/T 21 which acted as a sort of scout, and HMS *Philante* – once the private yacht of Sir Tom Sopwith but now the Despatch Vessel of CinC Western Approaches and acting as Headquarters ship. There were 'visitors' – the Canadian 9EG, on their way to Kola Bay escorting JW 67/RA 67, the very last Russian convoy, diverted to bring in five U-boats which were on passage from Trondheim to Loch Eriboll.

The object of the exercise was to disarm the boats as they came in, and to put boarding parties aboard in readiness for their eventual passage southwards to Loch Alsh. Each ship of 21st EG made three or four such trips escorting two or three U-boats at a time.

> See later in this chapter concerning HMS *Philante* and her presence with the 21st Escort Group. Accounts differ, but the differences are of a minor nature and they do not significantly compromise the accuracy of the record.

The Group arrived at the entrance to Loch Eriboll during the early morning of 9 May. We found the loch to be remote, deserted, rugged, grand; a sheet of water about ten miles long and a couple of miles wide at the mouth with the mountains of Sutherland tumbling into the background. We waited. The boarding parties drew weapons and rations – *Philante* arrived – the Motor Launch patrolled the entrance; and then, at half past nine on the morning of the 10th the first U-boat arrived, *U-1009*, on the surface, flying a tattered black rag from its periscope as a sign it was ready to surrender.

We launched our motor boat with the boarding party aboard.

> John Cunningham was an LTO – Leading Torpedo Operator. *Byron* did not carry torpedoes, so what was he doing? He was an electrician. In those days the torpedo branch looked after the electrics in a ship. John would have had torpedo experience and was probably responsible for the removal of the firing pistols from the U-boat's torpedoes.

4 BOARDING PARTY   *U-1009*. John Cunningham, LTO

As the motor boat approached the U-boat there was a heavy swell and it's no easy matter to come alongside a submarine at sea. The Cox'n said 'When I say jump, everybody jump.' I jumped and scrambled on to the casing on all fours, looked round, and found that I was the only one aboard! I looked towards the conning tower where I could see several men in leather suits, one wearing a white cap who I later discovered was the Kommandant. I walked very slowly towards them, reckoning that before I got there the rest of the boarding party would have caught up with me – which is what happened. Then we went through the Boarding Party drill. The German crew were ordered below, and our Officer, Buck Taylor, followed them. Myself and the Stoker shackled a chain to an upper deck stanchion and lowered it through the hatches down to the Control Room so they could not suddenly decide to dive. Two seamen with guns followed us, and a signalman. Two other seamen stayed in the conning tower. When we arrived in the Control Room the routine was for the officer to question the U-boat Captain, and for this purpose a questionnaire was supplied written in English and German: I can still hear Buck Taylor doing his best in a strong German accent, until the Captain suggested everyone might get on better in English.

We then took up our duties. Lt Taylor went forward to check for demolition charges and to see that the torpedo pistols were out, and I did the same at the other end of the boat. The Stoker and I then took up position in the engine room and the Battery Room, although neither of us were armed – the seamen in the conning tower had the only Lanchester carbines.

When we got under way and they started the diesel engines I could not believe the noise, it was horrendous. After a while I noticed that the German Engine Room Watch were giving each other hand signals and me dirty looks. I made my way slowly through the diesel room to where the Stoker was stationed and then took him into the Control Room and I asked him if he thought there was going to be trouble. Evidently he had experience on British submarines and he told me that they were only talking to one another in Deaf and Dumb language because of the noise of the engines.

At meal times the Germans lifted up the bilge plates and out came the tins of every conceivable luxury which we hadn't seen for years. It had been impressed on us not to accept food from the Germans and we had brought with us cardboard boxes of Field Rations which consisted of Corned Beef Biscuits and tins of tea, sugar and milk all in one. When we looked at our rations and what the Germans were eating it didn't take much of an invitation to join them.

We were given turns at going up on the conning tower for a breath of fresh air and although this was welcome the weather was rough and you needed the German wet weather clothing which included a heavy belt fitted with snap hooks so that you could attach yourself to a bar and prevent yourself being swept overboard. From time to time the U-boat went bows under and the conning tower filled up until it was like standing in a tub of water, but at least when it drained away you were still there! Under the conning tower in the control room was a rack containing some 40 or 50 pairs of binoculars and one man had the job of continually cleaning them and as one pair went off one end so others were cleaned and put on the other.

Halfway through the night we had a fault on the starboard engine and we had to stop whilst they sweated over the engines for some hours until the trouble was put right. (I don't think I would have bothered.) The engine room staff were certainly dedicated to their engines.

Next morning we arrived at Loch Alsh and took the boat alongside a submarine depot ship. The U-boat captain read out a message to his ship's company telling them that they were leaving their boat and I think there were a few tears.

We were picked up by our motor boat and returned to *Byron*.

5   THE PARTING SHOT – was a mistake

'We were under way, and I was on the conning tower with a couple of the Boarding Party and the U-boat Commander. Les Kingsley came up from below. We all had Lanchesters (a posh version of the Sten) and when Les came up on top he placed his Lanchester on the deck in an upright position, butt down. For no apparent reason a round went off, shot into the sky, missing the U-boat Commander's sleeve by a matter of what must have been 2–3 inches. He remained completely unmoved.' (Buck Taylor, Lieut: RNVR i/c Boarding Party)

It would seem that whoever fired the first shot in the Battle of the Atlantic, Les Kingsley fired the last.

6   LOCH ERIBOLL (Part II)

The need for a resident boarding party was never questioned, although the fact that most of the boats had made the passage, on the surface, from Norway, might have been taken as evidence of good intentions. However, an initial search of the U-boats was important as a Scapa Flow-type scuttling was a possibility, as were individual acts of last minute revenge. The search also included a general rounding-up of documents – log books, code books, signal and wireless manuals, signal files, official correspondence, charts, etc. Some boats were intact, some had ditched everything, most lay somewhere between the two. Whatever there was came back on board, usually in their thick, leather-strapped brown canvas folios, to be sent over to *Philante* the same evening.

Some souvenirs of the boats found their way on board. The grey 'wet suits' of course, and some cigars of such appalling quality that we actually felt sorry for their intended smokers; an immense quantity of naval issue writing pads came aboard; besides being decorated with the usual eagle and swastika, each one bore the reminder that the cheerfulness of the writer had a direct bearing on the morale of the receiver at home. I wrote an exceptionally cheerful letter to my Mother on such a piece and I regret to say that it alarmed her considerably.

For those of you who like a bit of detail to put things in perspective, thirty-three U-boats came into Loch Eriboll between the morning of 10 May and the evening of 19 May. The Group sailed south to Loch Alsh for the last time on 21 May escorting the last U-boats remaining in the loch. On 22 May the Group – less *Byron* – escorted four boats across to Moville (Northern Ireland); we came on alone a day later having waited in Loch Alsh to recover our boarding party. The Group as a whole then made a last entrance into Belfast.

7 THE U-BOATS

The boats which came into Loch Eriboll were, with a few exceptions, Type VIIC – the standard operational boat, and like all ships in all navies they differed one from the other.

U-532. You may remember the U-532: she was in fact a Type IXC, and therefore considerably larger than the Type VIIC, converted for cargo carrying, and arrived covered in barnacles and weed, with a cargo of tin, molybdenum, rubber, wolfram and quinine, having made the round trip to Japan. The Imperial War Museum have a collection of a dozen or so photographs of the *U-532* and her cargo. Those of her interior are the best photographs of living conditions aboard a German U-boat in the IWM's collection. The photographs are revealing: the U-boat itself is massive; but the seamen's mess, the PO's mess, even the Wardroom are cramped beyond belief and make *Byron*'s mess decks look palatial: a trip to the other side of the world in such conditions needed character. Also included is a Jolly Jack holding one of those dreaded Lanchesters, and a load of dockyard mateys fingering the cargo.

Her commander was something of a fanatic, convinced that Hitler was alive and that the 'surrender' was merely a ruse on his part so that Germany and the Allies could more effectively engage the Russians. Sir Max Horton inspected the *U-532* on arrival at Liverpool: maybe he wanted to see this phenomenon for himself.

Last June there was a dim echo of *U-532* – or rather a sister ship, *U-534.* This boat was sighted on the surface in the Kattegat between Denmark and Sweden on 5 May 1945 and sunk by a Liberator. *U-534* was raised about a year ago and taken to Denmark where she will go on display. She was armed with torpedoes, so it is unlikely that she was converted for cargo-carrying – although they did find 100 bottles of wine.

> *U-534* was later transferred to the UK and is currently on display for public inspection at Birkenhead.

U-1105. The one that had attacked and damaged *Redmill*. She was surprised to learn that her presence on that occasion had gone undetected.

U-1231. One of *Rupert*'s. This one was so full of wine that it was thought possible that she was acting as some sort of Off Licence to the entire German navy. Lt Black offered some of this to his sailors, but they sturdily refused to drink any of it; Captain (D) and the Belfast Customs, on the other hand, were evidently more understanding.

And the German navy? We found them to be sailors much like ourselves, well disciplined, responsive to the orders of their officers, and, even at the moment of surrender, with their morale intact despite the U-boat service having sustained casualties unsurpassed by any other fighting service.

8 'AND THE FIRST PAST THE POST IS . . .'

The rumour that 'our' *U-1009* was not the first U-boat to surrender started on 11 May 1945 and has lasted until now. The news was not well received on board, in fact I wrote home on the 11th, in pretty sharp terms:

'Whatever you may hear to the contrary you may take it from me that the first U-boat surrendered to this Group and what is more to this ship. We were the first by a good two hours ... several (U-boats) have come in. I can see one now, with our ensign over it while it is being searched. The crew are all on deck and conning tower sitting in their light green overalls and smoking.'

Our worst fears were to be realised, for *The Times* of Friday, 11 May 1945 shows a photograph of a U-boat with the following caption: 'The first of the U-boats to arrive at a British port was *U-249*. She surrendered to Commander W.T. Weir RN, seen here with Oberleutnant Koch on board the submarine.'

There the matter rested for fifty years, until we were confronted with the need to write this Newsletter and the necessity of finding out the truth. Alan therefore wrote to the MOD, Naval Historical Section.

We have their reply which, as one would expect, is helpful and informative.

The first boat to comply with Doenitz's signal was *U-1105*, which reported her position (from about 100 miles due west of Malin Head) at 0907B on 9 May. *U-1105* arrived at Loch Eriboll at 1830B on 10 May.

U-249 reported at 0922B on 9 May (from about 20 miles south of the Lizard) from where she set course for Weymouth. *Magpie* and *Amethyst* sighted her, and at 1600 hours *Magpie* went aboard her. She was escorted into Portland at 1100B on 10 May.

U-1009 reported at 1200B on 9 May (from between Shetland and the Faeroes). That afternoon she was attacked by mistake by an aircraft of Coastal Command, but continued on her surrender course to Loch Eriboll, being joined en route by *U-1305*. The two boats arrived at Loch Eriboll at 0815B on 10 May and were thus the first to enter a British harbour.

We therefore have three 'firsts', and you pays your money and you takes your choice.

U-1105 was the first to signal.

U-249 was the first to be boarded at sea.

U-1009 was the first to enter an Allied anchorage. (Actually an hour ahead of *U-1305*.)

9 LOCH ERIBOLL IN PICTURES

The Imperial War Museum has a collection of photographs taken at Loch Eriboll, and enclosed is a copy of one of them. It shows *U-1305* being boarded by a party from *Deane* and catches the feeling of what Loch Eriboll was like exactly. It is reproduced here with the permission of the Imperial War Museum, whose courtesy in allowing us to do so is much appreciated. (The original photograph is under their ref: A.28522).

10 A LETTER HOME

Cliff Greenwood wrote a letter home to his wife about Loch Eriboll, and his daughter, Sue Seabridge, has kindly allowed us to enclose a copy.

John Whithouse
Alan Hope

Relevant extracts from Cliff Greenwood's letter referred to in paragraph 10 are reproduced below. The need for continuing wartime secrecy and self-censorship is immediately apparent.

10 May 1945

We've made news – this time I wouldn't be surprised if we haven't made history – history with a capital H. And this time I think we'll be in the papers. There should be photographs too, for even as I'm writing this in the mess, official photographers are posted on a trawler at the mouth of an anchorage which was the scene of the morning's little operation, waiting to take pictures as we leave.

All the middle (watch) last night was tense, waiting for the developments which have made today's little exploit and no sooner had I gone on the forenoon (watch) today than I was called to the bridge to chronicle each incident for the captain who, I'm told, as soon as the operation began asked 'Where's my writer?' and had my name piped. It meant that Jock, who'd only just finished the morning watch, had to go on the forenoon. But I'd a seat in the front row of the stalls for a chapter in this war's aftermath which few men were privileged to see, watched it develop minute by minute, and will never forget it. She's only a little ship, this lass of ours, but she always seems to be there when the fun's on. Now, just before dinner, I've typed a report of four manuscript pages, the log's complete again and the captain who, I suspect, is making a scrap book out of these notes of mine, is as happy as a dog with a couple of tails.

14 May 1945   Monday   7.45 a.m.

Here is a little story I promised to you in an earlier letter. Here is the scene. It's the morning of May 10, VE Day plus 2. They've been celebrating the surrender ashore – we've heard them on the wireless. Otherwise the previous two days have been little different from any others to us except that the bread has gone stale on us, is speckled with sinister green spots and we're chewing biscuits and we've spliced the mainbrace and been given, a day late, a double ration of rum – neat too. We've rejoiced and been glad, or as glad as we can be. It's all over. It's so good to know it that we can't realise it. It was the same, I suppose, everywhere. The tension's gone and the inevitable reaction is setting in.

We've known for a day or two that after a certain prescribed hour all U-boats have to surface, put all armaments out of commission – torpedoes, mines, everything – and sail to certain anchorages to surrender. Our old enemies have to call it a day at last, have to admit defeat, the enemies we've been chasing and killing – four in one 10 day patrol – for months. Will they obey the order? We don't know. It's of no particular interest to us – it's sufficient for us to know that we've won the long, grim merciless battle – and it's been all that.

Then the signal comes. We've to go to one of the anchorages where they're to surrender. That makes us sit up! This is the day we've been waiting for. We sail for the remote isolated rendezvous, reach it in the late twilight, are disposed in position. Our little lass is given the honour, is told to wait near the mouth of the inlet as a trawler patrols outside in the open sea. Already the U-boats have begun to signal their positions according to the terms, every 8 hours. Two are approaching, should reach the inlet during the night, will wait outside for escort by the trawler until an hour before dawn before coming in – if they intend to come in. That's the question – will they come in?

The night passes. We know from our radar that one has reached the inlet mouth and is on the surface. What will he do? That again is the question. Is the battle still going on? Is he obeying orders? Or is he out on a suicide gamble? We wait. Early we go to action stations. I'm called to the bridge to act as writer. At least I've got a front row in the stalls. This is history, the first chapter yes, definitely the first, in spite of the BBC's report of the surrender at another anchorage – the first chapter in the mass capitulation of a fleet which was built to rule all the seas. The sun has lifted the mist from a sea as calm as a mill-pond, but the horizon is still hidden in haze. It's against this grey curtain that we see him – a long, black shape, low in the water, with a squat hump in the middle. Through the glasses you can see that she's flying a dark flag – it may be a blue flag – the flag of surrender. Near her the trawler is fussing, self-important, perky as a little terrier gambolling at the heels of a sullen quarry which refuses to play.

Far away, three miles astern, is another of those long black shapes – the second of them. In all the vast expanse of waters there's nothing else. Only the black smoke from the trawler's stack climbs into the clear morning sky. There is no other movement anywhere. And everything is so quiet – so quiet you can hear the gentle wash of the ripples against our bow. This is zero hour in the last act. The scene is framed in the great hills, range upon range of them, which border the inlet, hills russet-brown in bracken near the water's edge, fading into purple in the distance. There's a whitewashed cottage – a shepherd's cottage – standing beneath a bluff of rock on the far shore. As I watch through the glasses I see a man come out, a sheep dog prancing near him, and walk off and away up the hill without a backward glance. I see then, for the first time, that the cottage chimney is smoking. They've just had breakfast. It's just another day for them. They do say – some of the lads who've been ashore since – that when they met one of these shepherds and told him that the war was over and we'd won, he'd said 'Aye. I did hear tell that they'd beat that old perisher Napoleon'. But that's probably only a fable.

Now for it. It's 8 o'clock. They're at action stations everywhere. All guns are trained on the inlet mouth. The boarding party, armed with Sten guns and revolvers – and if the U-boat crew only knew it, half of them with revolvers could only hit a haystack in a passage if the haystack was very big and the passage very narrow – climb into a motor boat, squat there, cradled above the waters, waiting to be lowered. It would be just too bad for them if the U-boat suddenly bared her fangs. We've to take that chance. Slowly everything begins to move. 'Bring her in' is signalled to the trawler. Within a minute the long black shape is approaching. You can see the bow wave, crested with foam, which she lifts even in this quiet sea. She passes the mouth of the inlet, comes nearer and nearer, the trawler shuffling after her, but outside the line of fire – if we have to fire. Nearer she comes. You can see the length of her now, the lean ugliness of her, the rust stained brown on her black hull. You can see, too, a figure on the conning tower bridge. He wears a white jersey. There's a black peaked cap pulled low over his eyes. He's the first German I've seen, although I've been hunting them for months, for nearly six years. He seems to crouch on his perch. I train the glasses on him. As the U-boat comes nearer and nearer, on a course less than 200 yards inshore from our station, I see his face. It's not a face – it's a mask, expressionless, remote. That face will never betray his intentions.

Now the U-boat is almost level with us and reducing speed. 'Stop' we signal. She obeys. 'Lower Motor Boat.' Down she goes. The stutter of her engines breaks the silence. At that second, almost as if it's all been rehearsed, the hatch of the U-boat opens and two of the crew climb out, walk half a dozen yards forwards, wheel smartly and stand at the stand-easy position to face us. They wear brown overalls, are young – I can see that with the glasses – can see they've the faces of robots, blank, emotionless. I notice the flag then. It is blue. It is the surrender flag. We've got him – the first of the pack. The motor boat moves towards him in a wide half-circle, passes behind his stern, sweeps back, brushes alongside the low black hull. The two figures on the deck come abruptly to life, run aft, catch the mooring ropes. I see one of them stoop to help one of the boarders to the deck. It's over rapidly then. Each armed man races to his station. Up the ladder to the conning tower and the bridge the officer in command climbs fast. He reaches the bridge. For a split second I can see the two men face each other alone – the U-boat captain, the man in the white jersey, and the enemy who has come to take possession of his ship. Crisply, the Englishman salutes. The German acknowledges the salute with one of his own, which is a model of exactitude. It's all so strictly correct. But the guns are still trained, the guns' crews still at their stations. You never know with these Huns – you never know.

All we do know is that somewhere below decks the boarders are combing the ship and that the U-boat captain and the officer of the guard have gone with them, for the bridge is empty, the upper deck is empty and everything's gone quiet again, so quiet that again you hear the ripple of the tiny waves against our sides, and have time to notice that across on the other shore somebody has hung some washing on the line in the garden of the whitewashed cottage. It seems to last a long time but it's probably only a few minutes. Then up they climb to the bridge again and down the mast flutters the frayed blue flag, and up it the White Ensign, curling in a sudden gust of wind, fresh, clean, defiant. That's No.1 U-boat for Britain.

It's soon over after that. Still the guns are manned, but you know they'll not fire now.

The trawler is ordered ahead. She fusses into position, begins to steam down the water to the head of the inlet. After her churns the U-boat. After the U-boat we steam, down to the other waiting ships, bringing home the bacon. We've taken her out since – and another with her – to a base where they're assembling flotillas of surrendered craft and have come back again and soon we'll be out with another couple. They're all so compliant, so obliging, so courteous – the old Hun at his old games, arrogant in victory, servile in defeat. At the present rate of progress they'll soon be waiting in queues to come in. Definitely, in spite of the fact that there's not a pub within miles, no golden sands, no ballrooms, bands or baths, nothing but hills of heather and loneliness, this has become the most fashionable watering place for U-boats this spring. It's one of the most amazing stories in history.

Now I must do some work. Then, after breakfast, I've to type the report of the boarding party officer, who was dictating to me in his cabin until after midnight – and I was up again at 4 o'clock.

PS. As we were taking the first of our prizes in, a certain famous ship (HMS *Manxman* – a fast minelaying cruiser, doing about 30 knots! I was on the plot at the time. One never forgets. AH) signalled to us as she passed 'Glad you've got them at last just where you want them. You've put in plenty of sea time to deserve it.'

PPS Yes, these Germans are so compliant. They've only one concern. The first question ours asked was 'You won't give us up to the Russians please. Those Bolsheviks – they no good.' These Russians have got the daylights scared out of them.

PPPS Yes, ours was the first. The BBC gave the time of their reported first surrender at 11 o'clock. We were aboard at 8.15.

15 May 1945   Tuesday   11 a.m.

Only half an hour ago, so I'm told, while I was still helping as a cook to scrub out the mess, one of the officers came prowling in search of me again. I know what they were after – they wanted reports preparing and writing for the two who commanded boarding parties on our last two U-boats. I don't mind doing all this but when you're given no relief from two watches for doing it and seldom a thank you, and when I'd begun to suspect it's all being taken a great deal for granted, I'm beginning to agree with my boss that it's about time somebody said something. He said it today apparently. 'Now look here Sir', said he according to the version reported to me, 'this is alright, but you're wearing this fellow out. He's not as young as he used to be and he's tired. Do you know that he'd less than three hours sleep in 36 last week-end? Give him a break.' I'm told that this particular officer at once saw reason or decided it would be discreet to retire and retired with all the grace he could summon. Now when I passed the ship's office a few moments ago, they were all in a huddle working it out themselves. It will do them no harm.

17 May 1945   Thursday   1 p.m.

Another visitor today. He came in as quietly as ever. And again I'd a seat in the orchestra stalls. Now we're on our way escorting him to his last sanctuary. It's becoming almost a custom these days, but somehow it's not lost the first fresh excitement. All the time you're saying to yourself 'This is the end of a fleet that was to cut Britain's life-lines and starve her into surrender, and I'm seeing it.' It's a privilege and the familiarity has not seemed to make it anything else. The pity is that it's delaying our leave, for we have apparently come to be regarded not only as U-boat Killers No. 1, but as U-boat Collectors No. 1 too. The price that we have to pay is a delayed leave.

19 May 1945   Saturday   1.00 a.m.

I've just been out on the upper deck. We're at anchor again and a few of us are out of our bunks. No longer are all the doors bolted and barred. You can walk out now and take a breath of air whenever the atmosphere in the office becomes a little too sultry. The ships are no longer in darkness. Below, as I stand on the torpedo deck, I could see the glare of the lamp over the quarter-master's desk. Across the water the hills were dim shadows visible in the moonlight. There was a golden glow in one window. In all the others the lights had gone out long ago. But all the ship's lamps were winking at each another across the bay, and each lamp was mirrored in the still water. And high over the hills the star which I'd not seen for weeks shone all on its own.

It shouldn't be long now for leave for the customers are becoming fewer. U-boat Collectors Incorporated that's us. And we're to get medals too. I'll qualify for the 1939–1945 Star and probably for the Atlantic Star and there's a Russian Convoy decoration promised us by Old Joe (Joseph Stalin).

20 May 1945   Saturday(?)

It's not over yet. For they've just announced on the wireless that a positive armada of our old customers is expected to sail in in an hour or two, and once that happens I'll probably be called to the bridge. The press is here, quartered in one of the other ships. What a story – and because I'm in the Service I can't write it – and with all the inside information in my possession too. It's enough to make any newspaper man tear his hair out by the roots.

P.S. Now the boarding parties have been ordered to action stations. They must be coming in now – a whole flotilla of them. At least this is probably the last of them.

20 May 1945   Sunday [?]   10.45 a.m.

Only a few minutes ago I leaned over the side and talked to Harry, who is one of the men who boarded one of the 15 which sailed in to call it a day last evening. One of our little lassie's two was berthed alongside us. Every minute or two you can feel her bump against our side. As I talked to Harry on the submarine's bridge two Nazi officers were close to him, listening to every word we said and probably, for nearly all of them can speak English, understanding all we said. It was of no interest to them anyway. We talked, according to the non-fraternisation orders, as if they were not there at all, either invisible or so far beneath our notice that their presence could be completely ignored. That's what they hate – this contemptuous, casual indifference. Last night this lot all came on deck and snapped off a brisk Nazi salute. Nobody took the least notice of it. They might have been holding up their hands to ask if they could leave the room.

I cut the film last night to watch them come in. It was worth it. I can see a film any time. I'll never see this again. It was a lovely evening, the sun shining and a fresh wind rippling the waters of the loch. For half an hour I watched the open sea beyond the entrance. Then I saw the smoke of the escort vessels, our own escorts – last night we were not one of them – move into position and a few minutes later the familiar squat shape of the conning towers and, a little later still, the cream surge of the bow waves churned up by the submarines. It was incredible to see it – one after the other, each flying the White Ensign, they sailed past into the loch, a whole flotilla of them, nearer and nearer in a perfect unbroken line, wheeled each to its own anchorage and came back to rest for the night. You could see them scattered about the little bay, black shapes, lifting and falling in the little waves as I came off the first watch at midnight. That was the end of a fleet. All we have to do is deliver them to the authorities.

22 May 1945   Tuesday   2.45 p.m.

We're on the final lap now. Again we're a sort of Mary, but this time there are 15 lambs following us. They're still as meek as ever – on the surface. Yesterday morning, when I was on the 4 to 8 watch and had found the galley closed and was almost panting for a drink, I walked on deck just as dawn was breaking, hailed Harry, who I knew was on the bridge of our U-boat, and asked him what he could do about it. 'Come back in quarter of an hour' he said. When I returned he'd a pewter pot of hot tea prepared and so close was the submarine berthed alongside us that he was able to hand it over the rails to me, and with it a packet of ship's biscuits – and not the sort of biscuits we have to endure either, but sweet biscuits, crisp and fresh from a sealed tin. The world's turned upside down. We never imagined a week or two ago that we'd be drinking tea brewed in a U-boat galley and eating biscuits made for a U-boat's crew. It all seems crazy, but it's happening.

I can tell you now that we've been at Loch Eriboll, a small isolated loch on the north-west coast of Scotland, not far from the Isle of Skye. Three quarters of the U-boats to surrender have sailed in there. And it's been our group, selected, so we're told, because of our achievements in the last round of the U-boat war, which was chosen to meet them. From all parts of the Atlantic they've come, from Norway and, to escape the Russians whom they fear unashamedly, from the Baltic. Our grand total is about 30. And they've all packed in without a crack out of them. Now we're escorting the last 15 to another reception base. What will happen to them we neither know nor care.

Cliff Greenwood served on HMS *Byron* as Coder and was very much the father figure to the younger ratings aboard. He was at the time approaching 40 years old and prior to naval service had been an accomplished journalist, a fact which clearly shows in this very powerful piece of writing. These experiences were written down as they happened, and we are fortunate indeed that Cliff Greenwood's personal record has survived intact. A copy of the whole letter is lodged in the Imperial War Museum archives.

The following account, 'The Forgotten Operation' was written by Pat Godwin in July 2004 for inclusion in the America-based Destroyer Escort Sailors Association website (www.desausa. org) and is reproduced here by permission and with the sincerest gratitude. Pat Godwin sadly died in March 2006.

Pat Godwin, LTO, Destroyer Escort HMS *Fitzroy* (K.553),
Loch Eriboll, May 1945

Whilst all eyes were turned to the celebrations of VE Day on the 50th anniversary on 8 May 1995, one of the last operations of the war in Europe by the Royal Navy had, it seems, been forgotten.

As the war was drawing to a close at sea, after six horrendous years it was being run down. To this I refer to the war against the German U-boats. On 4 May 1945, U-boats were ordered to cease attacking and sinking ships at sea, the U-boats were also ordered not to damage or scuttle their boats in any way. This order, however, was disobeyed and many U-boats scuttled themselves in various harbours in Norway and Germany.

On 6 May 1945, all U-boats at sea were told to surrender themselves at British ports from 8 May.

On 6 May the 21st Escort Group, under the command of the then Lt Cdr Raymond Hart, DSCV and Bar, were in Milford Haven for refuelling after escorting a convoy into the Bristol Channel.

On 7 May shore leave was cut short and the ships of the group were ordered to sea. As yet we had no news that the war at sea was over and the group was ordered by Admiral Max Horton, DSO, C-in-C Western Approaches, to proceed to Loch Eriboll off the north-west coast of Scotland, to secure the anchorage and prepare for the surrender of the U-boats.

Loch Eriboll is a large lonely loch with sparse and rugged surroundings, with very few roads or houses, just a few crofts and hills. After a full-speed run the group arrived in Loch Eriboll on the early afternoon of 8 May. By this time, by an Admiralty signal we knew the war was over; not however for the 21st, although the ships of the group enjoyed the signal 'Splice the Mainbrace'.

The five ships were HMS *Conn* (K.509) - SO. 21st EG - Lt Cdr Raymond Hart, HMS *Byron* (K.508) - Lt J. Burfield, RN, HMS *Rupert* (K.561) - Lt Petrie Black, RN, HMS *Deane* (K.551) - Lt Cook, RN, HMS *Fitzroy* (K.553) - Lt Cdr O.G. Stuart, RCNVR. The C-in-C's yacht *Philante* joined the 21st on 9 May as a replacement [sic] for HMS *Redmill* (K.553) - Lt John Denne, RN, which had been torpedoed in Donegal Bay on the morning of 27 April 1945. She was laying up in Lisahally with 60 ft of her stern missing, and suffered 32 fatal casualties.

The first 'guard ship' was the SO HMS *Conn* which sent her motor boat loaded with an armed boarding party to await the first U-boat to come in; it was anti-climax – nothing was sighted! On the morning of 10 May, with *Byron* as guard ship, the first U-boat hove into sight. It was 0940 hours on a grey and dull morning, flying the obligatory Black Flag. *U-1009* crept slowly into the loch, the boarding party of Byron scrambled aboard to take the surrender and secure the boat. The Commander of the boat Korvettenkapitan Hilgendorf and his boat were escorted into the loch and anchored near *Byron*. All ships were on full alert until *U-1009* was made safe, no repeat of the Grand Fleet surrender of 1918 in Scapa!

Two more surrendered to the 21st on 10 May. The third was *U-1105* which surrendered to *Conn*. Korvettenkapitan Schwarz was the Commander who had tried to sink *Redmill*. It was the one and only operation that U-1105 had sailed on. The U-boats continued to come in at regular intervals over the next few days, with boarding parties having to be put on boats and then escorting them to Loch Alsh for complete disarmament, the crews taken off and the Officers on their way to PoW camps. The boats after cleansing, with a few German seamen left on board with the armed guards, were escorted over to their dispersal point at Lisahally where they would await their fate.

By 18 May, eighteen U-boats had surrendered in Loch Eriboll to the 21st EG, for the next few days nothing of note happened and the group were able to get themselves sorted out for it had been a hectic 8 days for them. On the night of 19 May a signal was received from the 9th Canadian EG of HMCS *Loch Alvie*, *Matane*, *Monnow*, *St Pierre* and *Nene*. They had been detached from returning from a Russian Convoy to make their way home. They had spotted a whole group of U-boats, took them over and escorted them to Loch Eriboll, turning them over to the 21st EG and the procedure of surrender was again set in motion.

At 1800 hours on 22 May, with *Philante* and *Byron* already in Lisahally, *Conn*, *Fitzroy*, *Deane* and *Rupert* escorted the last of the U-boats to their dispersal point; the escorts and ten U-boats arrived in the Foyle at 1630 hours on 23 May. Thirty-three boats had availed themselves of the surrender in Loch Eriboll, by far the largest number of seagoing U-boats to surrender in any one port in the UK. The 21st EG returned to their Belfast base for the last time.

The 21st EG had been involved in many incidents since they were first formed in August 1944 in Belfast. They were the first Captain Class Frigates to be used on a Russian convoy, later joined by 15th EG also out of Belfast. They sank four U-boats, three in 36 hours at the end of March 1945 and the first week in April. They were the last and youngest group formed for Western Approaches. As individual escorts they had taken part in Channel actions and the invasion on D-Day. Some had taken convoys through the Mediterranean. Their SO, Raymond Hart, had been CO of HMS *Vidette* (D.48) at the height of the Battle of the Atlantic and during the invasion was CO of *Havelock* (H.88). Previously he had seen service in the Mediterranean.

After his retirement from the Royal Navy, where he reached the rank of Captain, Hart was made a CBE to go with his DSC, DSO and Bar, and now 81 he lives in retirement at Southampton.

After the disbandment of the 21st EG in early June, *Conn*, *Byron* and *Fitzroy* were ordered to Norway to help in the relief of Bergen and joined the Victory Parade. A few months later, like many of these ships, they were returned to the USA where they were broken up. A pity, for they were excellent ships.

On their way to Lisahally on 21 May 1945 the following signal was received by 21st EG from Admiral Max Horton:

Signal to 21st EG. Number 2041. T/B/S/P/L. T/O/R 2015/21/5/45

'GOODBYE. MY MOST SINCERE THANKS FOR THE WHOLE HEARTED AND EFFICIENT CO-OPERATION YOU HAVE GIVEN. WHEN I KNEW I WAS COMING TO THIS JOB I ASKED FOR THE BEST GROUP THEY COULD FIND. I GOT IT. YOUR FINAL ESCORT OF TEN U-BOATS TO LISAHALLY IS A FITTING TRIBUTE TO YOUR CAREER IN WESTERN APPROACHES.' HORTON C in C WA.

Reply from 21st EG SO *Conn*:

YOUR EXTREMELY GENEROUS AND KIND SIGNAL IS MUCH APPRECIATED, WE ARE PROUD TO HAVE BEEN SELECTED FOR THIS JOB AND FORTUNATE TO WORK UNDER YOUR ORDERS, WE WILL DO OUR BEST TO DELIVER THEM SAFELY. HART *Conn* SO 21st EG, 21/5/45

U-boats surrendered to 21st Escort Group in Loch Eriboll

U-boat No. Depart Eriboll	Captain	Arrived Eriboll	Boarding Party	Escorted to Loch Alsh
U-1009 1300/10 May	Lt Hilgendorf	0940 10 May	Byron	Byron
U-1305 1300/10 May	Helmut Christiansen	1048 10 May	Deane	Deane
U-1105 0730/11 May	Lt Schwartz	1930 10 May	Conn	Rupert
U-1058 0730/11 May	Hermann Bruder	1700 10 May	Rupert	Rupert
U-826 1300/11 May	Cpt. Olaf Lubke	1745 10 May	Fitzroy	Fitzroy
U-293 1300/11 May	Lt Cdr Klingspor	0935 11 May	Fitzroy	Fitzroy
U-802 0700/12 May	Lt Cdr Schmoeckel	1445 11 May	Philante	Deane
U-1109 2300/12 May	Friedrich von Riesen	1500 12 May	Conn	Conn
U-825 1300/13 May	Lt Stolker	0730 13 May	Byron	Fitzroy
U-956 1300/13 May	Lt Ohling	0730 13 May	Byron	Fitzroy
U-532 2300/13 May	Cdr Junker	0730 13 May	Rupert	Rupert

U-boat No. Depart Eriboll	Captain	Arrived Eriboll	Boarding Party	Escorted to Loch Alsh
U-1231 2300/13 May	Cpt. Lessing	1330 13 May	*Rupert*	*Rupert*
U-516 2030/14 May	Cdr Wiebe	1400 14 May	*Fitzroy*	*Fitzroy*
U-1010 2030/14 May	Cpt. Gunther Strauch	1425 14 May	*Philante*	*Fitzroy*
U-764 0600/15 May	Lt H-K von Bremen	2000 14 May	*Fitzroy*	*Deane*
U-244 0600/15 May	Lt Fischer	2030 14 May	*Deane*	*Deane*
U-255 1200/17 May	Oblt Helmut Heinrich	0800 15 May	*Byron*	*Byron*
U-2326 1850/18 May	Lt Jobst	1200 18 May	*Fitzroy*	*Fitzroy*

The following U-boats were escorted into Loch Eriboll and turned over to 21st EG by Canadian 9th EG as above for disposal

U-boat No. Depart Eriboll	Captain	Boarding Party	Escorted to Loch Alsh
U-294	Heinz Schutt	*Loch Alvie*	9th EG
U-968	Lt Westphalen	*Matane*	9th EG
U-481 2000/20 May	Lt Andersen	*Monnow*	9th EG
U-997	Lt Lehmann	*Nene*	9th EG
U-716	Lt Dunkelberg(*)	*St Pierre*	9th EG
U-992	Lt Falke	MLS	
U-668	Lt von Eickstedt	*Byron*	*Conn*
U-1165 2000/21 May	Lt Homann	*Byron* (skel. 2)	*Fitzroy*
U-427	Lt von Gudenus	*Conn*	Caistor Castle
U-278	Lt Cdr Franze	*Philante*	Arrived Loch Alsh 0815 22 May
U-318	Lt Will	*Conn* (skel. guard)	
U-363	Lt Cdr Nees	*Deane*	*Rupert*
U-312	Lt CdrK-H-Nicolay	*Rupert*	*Deane*
U-313	Lt Schweiger	*Fitzroy*	*Byron*
U-295	Lt Wieboldt	*Fitzroy*	Arrived Loch Alsh 1000 (skel. guard) 22 May

Armed Guards transferred as follows:

Conn from *U-427* to *U-716*

Fitzroy from *U-313* to *U-992*

Deane from *U-363* to *U-1165*

At 1800 on 22 May *Conn*, Fitzroy, *Deane* and *Rupert* sailed for Londonderry escorting the following boats:

U-312

U-992

U-716

U-1165

Arriving at Lisahally, Loch Foyle 1630 on 23 May 1945

'Destroyer Escort' was a United States Navy designation – there was no such class in the Royal Navy. Only vessels equipped with torpedoes could be classed as 'torpedo boat destroyer', a designation going back to the late 19th century. These 21st EG ships were more correctly known as 'Captain Class Frigates', named after distinguished naval officers mainly from Nelson's time.

(*)   Oblt Hans Dunkelberg served as commander only to January 1945. He was superseded as commander in February 1945 by Oblt Jurgen Thimme, who surrendered the boat. See the data included in the Shaw/Donaldson narrative regarding the actions of the 9th (Canadian) Escort Group following.

The Russian convoys continued right to the end of the war and beyond. The final Murmansk convoy (JW 67) left the Clyde on 12 May 1945 escorted by the destroyers HMS *Onslow* (G.17) and HMS *Obdurate* (G.39) along with the 4th and 9th Escort Groups. HMS *Onslow* played a part later in the destruction of the surrendered U-boats.

On 16 May at 62 degrees 30 minutes North 04 degrees 05 minutes West the 9th Escort Group was detached to escort surrendered U-boats from Norway to Scotland for formal acceptance. This is the story of the 9th Escort Group's part in the largest U-boat group surrender, as seen by crew members of HMCS *Nene*.

The following account is an extract from the website http://timetraces.ca/*Nene*/ dedicated to recording the service and subsequent history of HMCS *Nene* (K.270); it is reprinted here with appropriate acknowledgement and gratitude.

Lt Cdr Eric Shaw and Sandy Donaldson, HMCS *Nene*, 9th Canadian Escort Group, Loch Eriboll, May 1945

The escort group EG 9, made up of HMC ships *Nene* (K.270), *Loch Alvie* (K.428), *Monnow* (K.441), *St Pierre* (K.680) and *Matane* (K.444) was steaming out of the mouth of the River Foyle leaving Londonderry, with orders to proceed to join the escort force, for Russian Convoy JW 67 outward and RA 67 homeward bound. Rumours of peace being imminent abounded as we sailed, as allied forces were at the gates of Berlin and we were expecting word momentarily that the war was at an end.

Actual message received by Frank Burton, telegraphist aboard the *Nene* at the war's end, whilst just off Narvik, Norway:

CONFIDENTIAL	MOST IMMEDIATE
ALL SHIPS	FROM ADMIRALTY

(1) THE GERMAN HIGH COMMAND HAS SURRENDERED UNCONDITIONALLY ALL GERMAN LAND, SEA AND AIR FORCES IN EUROPE. EFFECTIVE FROM 0001 B HOURS 9th MAY, FROM WHICH HOUR ALL OFFENSIVE OPERATIONS ARE TO CEASE. DUE TO DIFFICULTIES OF COMMUNICATIONS THERE MAY BE SOME DELAY IN THESE ORDERS REACHING ENEMY FORCES. ACCORDINGLY DANGER OF ATTACK BY INDIVIDUAL ENEMY SURFACE CRAFT, U-BOATS AND AIRCRAFT MAY PERSIST FOR SOME TIME TO COME.

(2) THE FLEET IN ALL WATERS IS TO REMAIN ON A WAR FOOTING AND IN A STATE OF CONSTANT VIGILANCE FOR THE MOMENT.

(3) SURRENDER PROCEDURE FOR U-BOATS WILL BE PROMULGATED SEPARATELY.

(4) NO (R) NO RELEASE IS TO BE MADE TO THE PRESS PENDING AN ANNOUNCEMENT BY HEADS OF GOVERNMENTS.

080012 B.

Here is the Canadian Press release printed in The Globe and Mail and the Toronto Star on May 23 1945:

15 NAZI SUBS 'CAPTURED' BY 5 CANADIAN FRIGATES
(Headline in The Globe *and* Mail)
15 SUBS 'BITE SOUR APPLE' YIELD TO CANADIAN FRIGATES
(Headline in the Toronto Star, *and printed in others, May 23 1945)*
By FRANK HEALY, RCNVR

Loch Eriboll, Scotland, May 22

Fifteen German submarines escorted by the five Canadian frigates which 'captured' them off the coast of Norway shortly after Germany surrendered May 7, have arrived at this picturesque port on the north coast of Scotland after a 500-mile journey, it was disclosed.

Also taken into custody was the commander of the U-boat flotilla, a Capt. Suhren, who wore the Iron Cross with Oak Leaves and said he was senior submarine officer on the Arctic Ocean and Barents Sea.

The U-boats were intercepted in the company of a German submarine depot ship and four merchant vessels. The enemy surface craft were ordered to steam for a Norwegian port, while the Canadian ships – *Matane, Loch Alvie, Monnow, Nene* and *St Pierre* – took up escort positions around the U-boats.

With Murmansk Convoy

The frigates, operating with a unit of the Home Fleet, were escorting a convoy to Murmansk when ordered to intercept a group of U-boats reported travelling south along the Norwegian coast.

'Our information was vague, but we opened up speed and covered about 270 miles before intercepting them', said Lieut. F.J. Jones of Montreal, commanding officer of the *Matane*. 'We could hardly contain ourselves when we sighted them about a mile off. We were at actions stations and ready to blast them out of the water. We signalled the depot ship and ordered all vessels to shut down their engines.'

The *Matane*'s executive officer, Lieut. J.J. Coates of Halifax, Petty Officer Massey of Verdun, Que., and Sgmn. William Parish of Port Arthur, Ont., boarded the German depot ship to accept the surrender. There they met Suhren, who said under order of the German High Command he was withdrawing his command from Narvik and proceeding to Trondheim.

Suhren added he would comply with Allied surrender terms, said all ammunition had been landed, that the German vessels carried no mines and that torpedoes had been rendered harmless.

'We warned them if they attempted to scuttle or submerge they would be destroyed and no mercy would be shown,' Coates said.

Suhren ordered the *U-278* to assume command of the submarine flotilla under the senior officer of the Canadian ships. He was permitted to send a signal to the U-boat crews, which read: 'Farewell, U-boats. We have worked well together. Don't be downhearted. Good-bye. Yours, Suhren.'

Before starting the long trip to Scotland an officer from the *Loch Alvie* Lieut Jacques Mallet of Montreal, and two ratings, LS Ben Sweezey of Winnipeg and Sgmn. Alfred O'Brien of Saint Joan, N.B., went aboard the *U-278* as liaison men.

'Between Lieut. Mallet's French and our sign language we made the Jerries understand our orders,' said Sweezey. 'The crew was friendly and at first seemed very scared. The three of us stayed on the bridge most of the time. The trip took two and a half days and it was so rough at times that we had to strap ourselves in the conning tower. We were soaking wet nearly all the time.'

As they neared the end of the trip, the *Nene* intercepted a signal from the *U-278* which it attempted to pass secretly to the other submarines.

The full text of this valedictory signal is quoted below in the context of the narrative from the *Nene*. Witnesses to the event claim that the U-boats were fully armed with torpedoes and mines at the time of surrender.

The 8:00 a.m. BBC news reported that Admiral Doenitz had ordered all U-boats to remain on the surface and to surrender. Germany surrendered and Escort Group 9 detached from the convoy on 16 May with orders to intercept the entire U-boat force based in Narvik Fjord. Those in Narvik numbered fifteen and they were accompanied by four service and supply vessels for the fifteen U-boats and a beautiful yacht with a German flag officer aboard. The King of Norway's yacht had been commandeered and was sailing under the German flag.

The enemy group was preparing to move to Trondheim when, on 17 May, two watch keepers and the captain sighted the tips of the masts and what appeared to be a ship's bridge on the horizon of the port bow of the *Nene*. All EG9 ships went to actions stations and proceeded at maximum speed to close the group. When we reached them we took up strategic positions and between us boarded several U-boats as a precautionary measure, checking them out.

The five surface craft were instructed to proceed to a Trondheim port. The remainder of the U-boats were to be escorted to Loch Eriboll on the north coast of Scotland. We had on board the *Nene* three crew members who were bilingual in English and German, whose parents had immigrated to Canada after the First World War and they were invaluable during the operation. The *Nene* monitored the U-boat W/T signals all the way back using our German-speaking crew members, one of whom was a W/T operator.

Sandy Donaldson was one of a detail of six that was instructed to go on board a German U-boat as a guard to take the submarine to the north of Scotland. They never slept for two days. There was little communication between our seamen and the German submariners because of language difficulties. Conditions were crowded in the submarine, with little space provided for the mess table and virtually no access on either side of the table. Sandy related that one of our seamen took his gun-belt off and told the German sailor to pass it to our other seaman located at the head of the table. Halfway up the table one of the German sailors removed the gun from its holster, looked at it and put it back in the belt and then passed it up to our seaman. It was a tense moment and an incident that is still vivid in his memory.

The following signal from the Senior U-boat officer to the group of submarines was intercepted and translated by Sonntag then transmitted by Sam Forsythe by signal light. It read as follows:

> Comrades, nearing England, we have to carry out a mission and obey the laws of their people. We have to obey the orders of our Fuehrer and take a bite of the sour apple. The weapons of our U-boats are out of commission. We only have to carry out this last mission of turning over our U-boats.

On arrival at Loch Eriboll on May 18 our EG9 group anchored and each ship was instructed to have a U-boat moored on either side. *U-992* came alongside on our port side and the whole U-boat crew were most co-operative and well-behaved and efficient. The U-boat captain (Hans Falke) spoke perfect English having been partly educated in Britain, primarily for a business career. He was twenty-five years old! His crew frequently asked for any one of your German-speaking lads, amongst them Bruno Sonntag, to come on deck and answer questions on Canada, including how so many German speaking people got there.

U-295, carrying the German Fleet Commander, coming alongside punched a hole in *Nene*'s starboard side, three feet above the waterline at Seamen's Mess Deck. Two seamen were slightly injured. Art Desjardine, the shipwright, rigged a plug inside the mess area, with lumber and canvas to prevent taking in water during open water operations. The German captain claimed that the whole incident was an unfortunate accident.

This U-boat Captain's behaviour was sloppy and erratic. He was told to come aboard the *Nene* with a list of his boat's requirements, if any, to enable them to get to Loch Alsh for internment. When he came on board he gave a Nazi salute. He was told to get right back on board his U-boat and come on board properly or disciplinary action would be taken against him.

We sailed from Loch Eriboll on May 19th with the U-boats and arrived at Loch Alsh on May 20, where we turned them over for internment. We then proceeded to Londonderry.

It was quite a sight to see these U-boats waiting to surrender just outside the harbour as the dawn broke over the horizon.

The *Nene* made her last trip down the Foyle River past U-boats tied up at Lisahally, to bid farewell to Londonderry. On May 27 1945 *Nene* headed for Sheerness on the Thames and after some heavy scrubbing and painting from the bilges up, she was returned to the Royal Navy and accepted into reserve category 'B' at Sheerness on June 11 1945.

Some seven years later, Captain Shaw received a letter from the skipper of *U-992*. He said that when he arrived home there was a great deal of chaos in Germany. He told his wife how friendly the Canadians seemed at the surrender. As they both spoke good English, they decided to emigrate to Canada, if and when possible. They were eventually successful and settled into farming north of Winnipeg. They were doing well and had two sons born in Canada.

Most of the crew returned via troop train to HMCS *Niobe* in Greenock to await the passage home. Part of the final message read:

> Special train leaves Sheerness at 1335 arrives Nottingham 1930 departs 1950 arrives Greenock 0615/3. One bagged meal and one meal order will be issued to each rating on the train at Sheerness. Hot tea and a meal will be supplied in Nottingham. Mugs are to be carried.

We packed our mugs as ordered for the trip to the naval base HMCS *Niobe*, at Greenock, Scotland. Each of us was in very good spirits (Pusser's), compliments of our supply assistants Ceo Gaudet and Gene Begin. Serge Breard, our Sick Bay Attendant, supplied us with medical supplies in case of incidents during the trip. As our troop train proceeded from the south of England to Scotland there were many children at the station stops, all voicing admiration for the Canadians. 'Any gum, chum?' 'Any Spam, Sam?' We had ample supplies, so we dispensed gum, chocolate bars, to them as thousands of Canadian Army and Air Force had done during the six years war.

For many of us the adventure was the first time we had ventured more than a few miles from home. We had not seen our country, let alone the vast ocean we found ourselves on. It led one to think about the universe, the order of things and the magnificence of the ocean. It gave us time for reflection and thought, why we were there.

Reduced to category 'B2' reserve in December 1946 the *Nene* was towed to Harwich in May 1947 and transferred to Barrow-in-Furness in May 1953. Approval to scrap was given in June 1955 and on 18 July 1955 she left Barrow under tow of the breakers, T.W. Ward Ltd, to be broken up in Briton Ferry, Wales in August 1955.

List of German submarines and supply vessels surrendered to EG9 task force on thursday May 17 1935

U-Boats in two groups as indicated (*) = escorted by HMCS *Nene*

No.	Morse Name	U-Boat No.	Kmdt	No.	Morse Name	U-Boat No.	Kmdt
1	UANC	278	Franze	1	UBGA	668	Henning

No.	Morse Name	U-Boat No.	Kmdt	No.	Morse Name	U-Boat No.	Kmdt
2	UAQT	363	Nees	2	UAOP	313	Schweiger
3	UANV	295	Wieboldt (*)	3	UAWX	481	Andersen
4	UBTC	968	Westphalen	4	UBID	716	Thimme
5	UANT	294	Schutt	5	UATN	427	Gudenus
6	UBVD	992	Falke (*)	6	UBVI	997	Lehmann
7	UCDQ	1165	Homann	7	UAOV	318	Will
				8	UAON	312	Gazen

SUPPLY VESSELS

No.	Morse Name	Ship Name
1	DXE	*Grille*
2	WHG	*Huascaran*
3	DKM	*Kamerun*
4	SP	*Stella Polaris*
5	TRG	*Karnten*

The 'Morse Name' radio call signs listed immediately above were allocated to the German vessels by the Allies after capture. Kriegsmarine vessels, of course, did have individual call signs, but they were always of three characters only. That identifying *U-992*, for instance, was XUL.

Lieutenant Commander Eric R. Shaw, RCN (or 'Skipper', as he was affectionately known to the crew of the evidently happily efficient HMCS *Nene*) also contributed an expanded version of his part in the arrest of the surrendering U-boat flotilla off the Norwegian coast to *The Real Cold War*, a book relating the privations of the British naval force posted to the Russian naval base at Polyarnoe, on the north Russian Arctic coast, in order to set up and man a communications centre there. This signal station was the principal radio traffic route between the British Admiralty and the Russian base co-ordinating the Arctic convoys. Details of this publication are listed in the bibliography of this book. Shaw's second narrative follows below.

Lieutenant Commander Eric R. Shaw, RCN

Escort Group 9, five Canadian frigates, one being my ship, left Londonderry to join the escort force for Convoy JW 67 out and RA 67 homeward. Rumours of peace being imminent abounded as we sailed, Allied forces being at the gates of Berlin and were expecting this long and real Cold War to end at any moment. At 0800 on VE Day altering course to take position in our group my first lieutenant came with haste and speed to the bridge to report:

'Captain, 8.00 a.m. news on the BBC states Admiral Doenitz has ordered all U-boats to remain surfaced and to surrender.' Signals were sent for instructions on what should happen in view of the BBC announcement. 'Proceed as original instructions; further will be sent.' Then a signal from an unidentified escort:

'Am attacking bogey U-boat contact intend to continue until ordered otherwise.' Then the final signal for 'All systems go'. 'Proceed north to position off Trondheim, Norway, to take over surrender of all U-boats, tenders and accompanying vessels.'

So it was goodbye to JW and RA 67 – we were on our own, with a special mission, with great excitement, yet on guard for possible problems.

At 0230 on May 17 the U-boats were sighted. We all went to action stations and at maximum speed to close the group. On reaching them took up strategic boarding as a checkout procedure. A noticeable minority showed semblance of hostility, but most were philosophical, many being glad it was all over. There were twenty craft in all, four supply vessels and a beautiful yacht belonging to the King of Norway with a German flag officer on board. The surface craft were instructed to proceed to a Norwegian port. They desperately wanted to come with us as unless they were to surrender to the Norwegians they would be taken by the Russians and in view of the horrors their armies had inflicted on the Soviet people, very little mercy would be shown.

We then put a communications officer and two ratings on board the German senior officer's boat and set course for home; but not quite so simple, as things began to happen. On board *Nene* we had three crew members who were bilingual in English and German so were invaluable during the voyage.

They came peacefully enough, although one, more defiant than the rest, flaunted a skull and crossbones painted on the black flag of surrender.

The sleek and powerful yacht and the four depot ships having been despatched to Norway, the U-boats under our command were in two columns, line abreast with engines stopped. With our crews at action stations and still at weapons manned, in case they were not as innocent as they seemed, we threaded our way through the columns to interrogate and ascertain they had complied with surrender. German officers crowded the conning towers dressed in seagoing best, prepared to be dumb; evasive smiles and shrugs of the shoulders greeted our questions as we neared the U-boats: you could feel the hostility in the air.

These former terrors of the deep, the U-boats crews – although friendly, seemed very scared. Others were smiling, treating it all as a joke amongst themselves.

The convoy got under way in two columns, the U-boats bunched together as close as safe navigation allowed with the frigates patrolling up and down the wings. As night came we ran into a storm and as the weather deteriorated this caused problems. The conning tower staff and the boats took a bashing, and were forced to submerge. Surfaced submarines can stand just so much and no more, appearing to be under water as often as on the surface with tons of water pouring down the conning tower hatches. Constant watch was needed, fearful that if we looked away one of our charges would go missing.

The suspicion was aroused when one asked permission to submerge to make a minor repair owing to bad weather, but surfaced within the allotted time.

A rumour, 'a buzz around the ships' stated that prior to sailing from Norway the skipper of *U-992* was ordered to wear full uniform until further orders. This meant that he was to be tried for treason, the charge being 'For severe derogatory remarks about Hitler' in the presence of an undercover Gestapo agent amongst the U-boat crew. For this reason he was the happiest man in the group to get to sea. When the surrender order was issued it blew the Gestapo member's cover. The rumour continued, and when the U-boat asked for permission to submerge to correct a problem the crew member was ordered forward to check if the gun was properly secured. Whilst he was there the U-boat submerged, leaving the Gestapo agent to a fate he had consigned to others.

We could almost feel sorry for these beaten enemies, so close to or in the soaking cold water as even we were 'shipping them green over the bridge'. Nevertheless we were constantly on the look-out for treachery and the possibility that one or two with more venturesome spirits might make a bolt for it, or even the fanatical Nazis might attempt to scuttle their craft in spite of the cold water.

On arrival at Loch Eriboll on the 18th EG9 group, each escort was instructed to have a U-boat on each side; their crews were co-operative, well-behaved and efficient. The captain, 25 years old, spoke perfect English. I had tea with him in the conning tower: in return he had breakfast with me aboard the *Nene* to discuss his trip to Lochalsh for internment with his other officers and U-boat crews. He was beaming when told they would be home in six weeks.

Unlike the commander of the U-boat on our starboard side who thoroughly spoilt the relationship by putting a two-foot gash in our hull – either by design or sloppy handling or still bitter to the end. We had difficulty with him, a dyed-in-the-wool Nazi.

The situation was still tense, even more so when he came aboard and gave a Nazi salute. I told him to get back on his boat and come aboard my ship properly or I would take disciplinary action. To improve his manners, one of our petty officers offered, if I gave the order, to throw him in the salt chuck, but a threat of a cold bath in Scottish waters changed his attitude. He was so brain-washed he found surrender hard to accept.

Prior to this final incident and approaching the end of the arduous voyage, before entering harbour came relief and reassurance of all previous problems, as signals were being sent in 'plain language'. HMCS *Nene* intercepted a most heartening message from the senior officer of the U-boats:

> Comrades nearing England we have to carry out a mission and obey the law of their people. We must obey the orders of our Fuehrer and take a bite of the sour apple. The weapons of our U-boats are out of commission. All that remains for us is to carry out this last mission and turn over our gallant U-boats. Franze.

They followed us into port like lambs.

Howard R. Elliott (Hamilton, Ontario) Crew Member, HMCS *Nene*,
Northern Ocean and Loch Eriboll, May 1945

I signed up for the Canadian Navy in 1943 and following basic training and signal school in Quebec I was posted as Visual Signalman to HMCS *Nene* along with fellow Sigs Ron Graham and Sam Forsythe.

During our voyage escorting the U-boats from Norwegian waters the following signal was issued, which indicates just how twitchy things were until we reached the safety of the British anchorage:

TO: *Monnow*   FROM: EG9

A CONTINUOUS AND MOST CAREFUL WATCH IS TO BE KEPT ON ALL BOATS. IF THERE IS ANY ATTEMPT TO DIVE OR ABANDON SHIP FIRE IS TO BE OPENED AT ONCE. S.O. OF DIVISIONS ARE TO APPORTION RESPONSIBILITY AFTER WHICH EACH SHIP CAN STATION ITSELF AS IT THINKS BEST KEEPING AT POINT BLANK RANGE WITH ONE GUN TRAINED.

I well remember our entry into Loch Eriboll escorting fifteen arrested U-boats. *U-295* and *U-992*, being unable to anchor, were moored alongside. I also recall the incident where the commander of *U-295* came aboard the *Nene* in answer to a request that he provide a list of requirements to enable his boat to be taken onwards to Loch Alsh, and him flashing a Nazi salute. This was the same U-boat captain who had, just previously, holed our ship whilst coming alongside to secure. His greeting was, in the circumstances, not calculated to impress our skipper, and he was promptly returned to his boat with the instruction and implied threat that he had better try again, properly, or he would be dealt with!

With *U-295* moored alongside we had the opportunity to go aboard her, a combination of natural curiosity and an overwhelming desire to satisfy the souvenir-hunting instinct. Sam Forsythe and myself spotted an officer's white cap on a desk in a small cubicle, which Forsythe attempted to tuck into his jumper as a fair spoil of war. The cap was not too well concealed.

As we headed up the ladder into the conning tower, me following Forsythe, my head hit the soles of his boots when we came to an abrupt stop. Standing in the conning tower and staring down through the hatch at us, severely, was *U-295*'s Commander Wieboldt (though we did not know his name at that time), motioning us back down into the U-boat with the hat. And that was the end of that souvenir. Wieboldt might have been a captured combatant, but he was still captain of his vessel and he was determined that our thieving expedition would be terminated without success.

And another amusing incident during our brief stay aboard *U-295* happened as we were negotiating the control room beneath the conning tower. One of the German crew motioned to us indicating that he had something to show us. He produced the U-boat's log and pointed to entries which included *Nene*'s pendant number K.270 – on a couple of occasions they had spotted and identified us whilst submerged, and had recorded the contacts. Speaking German, and with exaggerated hand gestures, he was intent on describing our attack on his boat.

Putting his fingers to his lips – indicating quiet silence - then transferring his cupped hands to his ears indicating– indicating listen listen - he then said

'Was ist das?'

'Wasser bombe' (Depth charge)

'Kaboom' (Universal language and no need for translation)

He then mimed the crew looking around the boat, inspecting for damage. No damage was found, which prompted the crewman to burst into loud, loud laughter. 'Ha, ha, ha', he acted out several times, with rising volume and increasingly hearty slaps on the back.

A signal from our skipper (Captain Shaw) to the Group Commander later expressed his frustration at the depredations of the Royal Navy personnel amongst the U-boats, and the hopes of perhaps better times to come:

TO: CO (EG9)   FROM: CO (*Nene*)

WE GOT PRACTICALLY NOTHING. THE RN BOARDING PARTIES LOOTED OUR U-BOATS LIKE A BUNCH OF THUGS EVEN TAKING SOME PERSONAL GEAR. TWO OF US GOT HELMETS AND BADGES BUT NO BLONDES. HOPE FOR BETTER LUCK IN DERRY.

We did not know it at the time, though we later heard about Wieboldt in action on a previous convoy mission and were aware of his attacking expertise. Escorting convoy RA 61 just off the Kola Inlet off the north Russian coast, *U-295* fired a T5 GNAT (Giro Navigational Acoustic Torpedo) into a sister frigate HMS *Mounsey* (K.569).

HMS *Mounsey* was a lease-lend Captain Class (originally Evarts class DE 524) frigate built in the Boston Navy yards in 1943. The attack took place on 2 November 1944 and *Mounsey* was able to limp into the Kola Inlet for temporary repairs. There were many casualties. *Mounsey* returned to UK later along with our convoy RA 62 for permanent repairs to be carried out. She survived the rest of the war and was sold on 8 November 1946 for scrap to the North American Smelting Company.

I found it very strange that those same eyes that motioned us back down the ladder into the U-boat in May 1945 were the same eyes that just a few months earlier had been peering through the periscope and preparing to attack our convoy. It was *Mounsey*'s misfortune that she was selected and we were spared.

The (mis)fortunes of war!

It is quite enlightening to compare the separate views of these events as seen from the perspective of the British crews of the 21st Escort Group and their Canadian counterparts of the 9th. It has to be said that there was a certain measure of simmering discontent between the two factions, before, during and after the events in Loch Eriboll, and this will be described and partially explained later in this chapter.

But first I will, by way of explanation, attempt to clarify one or two annoying little anomalies which appear to have arisen between the narratives compiled by the respective ships' crew members. And finally I will expand on how the fourteen U-boats which left Norway with the 9th (Canadian) Escort Group became the fifteen which arrived in Loch Eriboll!

First, the question of the King of Norway's yacht, confusion over which features more than once in the foregoing narratives. There was in fact no Royal Yacht used by the Norwegian Royal family prior to the Second World War. Briefly, the circumstances were that in 1905 Norway formally seceded from Sweden to become a separate sovereign state. When the Norwegian Government invited Prince Carl of Denmark to take the vacant throne, part of the agreement was that a Royal Yacht would be provided for the Sovereign's use. Prince Carl agreed, taking the name King Haakon VII, but due to the new nation's difficult economic position after the dissolution of the union the new king did not call upon the Government to provide the yacht.

King Haakon, as a former career naval officer, would no doubt have had his own sailing vessel which sufficed for his immediate needs until the national situation permitted provision of the promised Royal Yacht. But a steady and continuous deterioration in the world situation culminated in 1940 with the invasion of Norway, and the question lost all importance. So there was no Norwegian Royal Yacht on the outbreak of the Second World War, and therefore no such vessel could have been requisitioned by the invading forces.

In 1927 the Bergen Line of Norway commissioned a luxury cruise liner which, as the *Stella Polaris*, became one of the most luxurious vessels in the inter-war years. On the fall of Norway this vessel *was* requisitioned by the German authorities and used as a U-boat crew rest and recreation facility until 1943. Thereafter the vessel was used as a troop ship, retaining the name *Stella Polaris* throughout.

When the 9th Escort Group happened upon the formation of surfaced U-boats and accompanying supply vessels on 16 May 1945, *Stella Polaris* was the most prominent of these support ships, and I suggest that it was this vessel which was assumed by the arresting ships' crews to be the King of Norway's yacht. I can see quite how the erroneous assumption came to be made – with her clipper bow, sleek lines and elegant profile, the *Stella Polaris* would be every man's impression of how a royal yacht should look. And of course the vessel may have been referred to as 'The Royal Yacht' by her German crew, possibly to deflect attention away from the former Fuehrer vessel.

Each of the other four surface vessels accompanying the surrendering surfaced U-boat group is positively identified and, except in the case of the one slight possibility following, could not have been confused with a supposed Royal Yacht. These four vessels were: depot ship *Huascaran* (6,951 gross registered tonnes, built in 1939 as a German passenger/cargo ship for the Hamburg-America Line); repair ship *Kamerun* (5,042 grt, built 1938 as a German cargo ship for the Woermann Line AG, Hamburg); fleet oiler *Karnten* (7,000 grt, completed in 1941 – laid down in 1939 as a Dutch fleet oiler); and fleet tender *Aviso Grille* (2,560 grt, completed in 1935 for the Kriegsmarine, which eventually became Adolf Hitler's personal yacht, although infrequently used by him. This vessel served as HQ to the FdU, Norwegen (C-in-C, Norway) during the war.)

As a further aside, three of these support vessels were, later in 1945, despatched to Loch Ryan loaded with spares in order to keep the impounded German U-boat flotilla in running order whilst awaiting its fate. The *Huascaran*, the *Kamerun* and the *Karnten* were joined by the *Neumark* as depot ships servicing the captured U-boats; the majority of the U-boats were destroyed and the depot ships later returned to Germany.

The one remaining vessel of the five accompanying the surrendering U-boats intercepted by the 9th Escort Group was the depot ship and former cruise liner *Stella Polaris* of 5,209 grt. My proposition is that this vessel was and has been for the whole of the post-war period erroneously identified as the King of Norway's yacht.

There is the possibility of course that the *Aviso Grille* might have been assumed by the Canadian personnel of the 9th Escort Group to have been the former Norwegian Royal Yacht, but I tend to discount this theory. Hitler's former yacht was by far the smaller of the two royal yacht candidates – half the size in fact – and, though presenting rakish lines and the classic luxury yacht profile, would certainly have appeared the lesser of the two when approached at speed and at some distance from the open sea. I accept that my proposition is based on supposition and speculation, but until unimpeachable corroborative evidence is forthcoming I am satisfied that it presents the strongest likelihood.

Only in 1947 was the question of the Norwegian Royal Yacht readdressed. For the fascinating story of this vessel, which coincidentally had a significantly close connection with the surrender of the U-boats to Loch Eriboll, see the postscript following.

Secondly, it is clear from the memoirs of Commander A.N.C. Layard, officer commanding the 9th Escort Group from HMCS *Matane* that two U-boats arrested by the 21st Escort Group and escorted into Loch Eriboll in the early afternoon of 14 May had already been stopped by their Canadian counterparts earlier that day. Layard records that when, on 14 May, his escort group with convoy JW 67 was to the north of Britain he encountered, unexpectedly, two surfaced U-boats flying black surrender flags heading towards Scotland. He detached HMCS *Matane* and HMCS *St Pierre* to intercept the two U-boats and escort them well clear of his convoy. He then rejoined and continued with his convoy escort duty, presumably after having advised the British naval authorities of the presence of the two enemy vessels then approaching Loch Eriboll. The 21st Escort Group accepted these two U-boats some hours later. The individual service records of *U-516* and *U-1010* in section one of the individual U-boat data reflect these events.

Thirdly, the circumstances of the simultaneous arrest of fifteen U-boats are detailed by Commander Layard. Two days after his encounter with the first pair of surfaced U-boats he was advised that a German convoy had been reported off the Norwegian coast, and the 9th Escort Group was detached to investigate. What he found was a formation of two columns comprising fifteen U-boats, with five surface ships in attendance. The story of the arrest of these U-boats is adequately covered in the Shaw/Donaldson narrative. Layard does, however, add a little more colour to the story as told from the crew members' viewpoint.

Layard names as the German officer in charge of the surrendering group one Suhren, and the dealings between those two principal opposing naval officers add a revealing insight into the tensions of the time. Reinhard ('Teddy') Suhren was a very senior career naval officer, then FdU, Nordmeer, or, as Layard describes him and his position, Commander-in-Chief of the German Arctic and Barents Sea Command. He had commanded *U-564* between April 1941 and October 1942, during which time he sank or damaged 125,000 tons (23 ships) of Allied shipping. He was at the time of his arrest holder of the Knights Cross with Oak Leaves and Crossed Swords, a veritable U-boat 'Ace'.

The sparring between the two naval commanders reflects the highly charged nature of the occasion. Layard pointed out the severe consequences for any U-boat captain considering scuttling his vessel. Such an act would result in the immediate destruction of the boat, and no mercy would be extended to the crew. Layard then ordered Suhren to accompany the five surface ships to Trondheim whilst the fifteen U-boats would be escorted by the 9th Escort Group to British waters. Suhren resisted this order on the grounds that it countermanded his own orders. In the ensuing stand-off Layard remained adamant and refused to give Suhren his name and rank when these details were demanded. Suhren was placated only when given *Matane*'s pennant number and an assertion that these new arrangements would be relayed to Allied Command. Command of the U-boat flotilla passed to *U-278* under Lt Cdr Franze and Suhren headed for Norway.

Fourthly, Suhren must have soon been returned for imprisonment and debriefing, as interviews with him were published in the British press.

Fifthly, the intriguing suggestion in the second Shaw narrative of how the unmasked Gestapo agent aboard *U-992* was summarily dealt with. It has to be made clear at the outset that the events described, whilst having some ring of truth with regard to the peculiar circumstances pertaining at the time, are unlikely to have happened as described. It may well be that similar events did occur on other boats where crews recognised opportunities for revenge, but as for *U-992*, this is unlikely, for a number of reasons.

The principal problem is with the forward deck gun on *U-992*. Deck guns were fitted during the earlier years of the U-boat war, but as the threat of air attack increased guns were gradually removed. The main difficulty was that there was just insufficient time to secure the deck gun and to recover the gunners safely below deck in a crash-dive situation. *U-992* was a Type VIIC boat commissioned in August 1943; from her launch she did not carry a forward deck casing gun, a fact confirmed by photographic evidence obtained at the time of her surrender in Loch Eriboll.

The alleged Gestapo agent could not therefore have been ordered forward to secure the deck gun, and thus could not have been left to the sea when the boat submerged. He might just have been ordered to attend to the bridge guns, but in that case there would have been sufficient opportunity for him to descend the conning tower hatch when it became apparent that the boat was submerging. Unless, that is, the hatch was secured from below whilst he was outside, in which case he would have been aware immediately, as would the majority of the remaining crew members. And no such story ever surfaced during the crews' years in captivity.

But it is a colourful story and one which may be worthy of further research. It is, perhaps, one of those tales which has been embellished with every retelling, from a grain of truth developed elsewhere in different circumstances.

Sixthly, relations between the German crews and the Canadian boarding parties were courteous but without any show of friendliness, according to Layard, who records that the passage to Scotland was mostly uneventful, although he did suspect that some of the mechanical problems reported by the U-boats may have been fabricated. He issued a short, sharp warning that any delaying tactics would result in extended detention in the UK prior to repatriation, which immediately solved the problem. *St Pierre* was required to escort two U-boats into Shetland for fuel. They rejoined the remaining captives in convoy and all were handed over to the naval authorities in Loch Eriboll.

Layard records with some pride that the 9th Escort Group's personnel were entirely proper in their dealings with the captive crews and vessels – they did not resort to looting, unlike some of the 'sharks' in the Scottish ports. This seems to have been a further reflection of the antipathy between the Canadian and British crews, and there was some history of friction dating back to a period much earlier in the war.

In Loch Eriboll, as ships of both escort groups lay in the midst of a dense fog, one of the prizes berthed alongside *Monnow* was boarded by Royal Navy personnel from one of the British frigates. The visiting launch then became disorientated in the fog and, following an engine failure, drifted alongside *Monnow*. The crew of the launch were determined to leave and displayed some anxiety when denied permission to do so because of the fog. Surprisingly they posted an overnight guard on their launch. After their engine was repaired the next morning they departed in some haste before *Monnow*'s crew discovered that one of the U-boats berthed alongside had been picked clean, including a case of brandy known to have been aboard the previous day. *Monnow*'s crew were understandably furious when they learned later that the clandestine overnight visitor carried the loot, but by then it was much too late to regularise matters.

The 9th Escort Group departed that day, 21 May, for Loch Alsh, where once again the U-boats were handed over to yet more local naval authorities. The local officer-in-charge criticised Canadian personnel for fraternising with the enemy. Layard accepted that the censure had merit, though he noted that the German crews wholly accepted the terms of the surrender without question and his crews had been sailing with their former enemies for five days. He conceded that it was 'indeed difficult to prevent English and Canadian personnel from displaying small acts of kindness or goodwill'. He took the view that perhaps showing kindness towards all of those who had endured the rigours of the Atlantic campaign was a fitting way for reservists, British and Canadian, to end the war.

Don Delong, a member of the crew of HMCS *Nene*, related that the ship left Londonderry on 27 May and headed for Sheerness on the Thames. After the frigate was thoroughly scrubbed, painted from the bilges up, made ship-shape and inspected prior to being handed back to the Royal Navy, many of the Canadian crew threw paint on the walls, and trashed the mess and other parts of the ship as payback for the disgusting condition in which the ship had been delivered to them in Halifax. He described his first view of the *Nene* as a 'disgusting pig-sty'. In fact the ship's complement was not allowed to bunk on board for two weeks, spending their daytime hours in Halifax cleaning the ship.

In Sheerness at the end of the war many of those items that would have been valued today – stainless steel cutlery, china, etc, anything not nailed down – lay at the bottom of the harbour. All was not well between the Allies during the war. The colonials (Canadians) felt slighted. This is further substantiated by Don's arrival at an earlier posting on HMCS *Ettrick*. She too was soiled with food items like ketchup and butter thrown about by the Brits: all very sad, really.

And finally, the definitive solution to a problem that has exercised researchers over the years: what was the total number of U-boats intercepted off the Norwegian coast on 16 May

1945 and escorted to Loch Eriboll, and exactly how many, and which, were received and processed there three days later?

A close examination of the surviving documentation reveals that there really should have been no question concerning the numbers involved, though over the years fourteen, fifteen and sixteen have been quoted as the total of U-boats intercepted in Norwegian waters and escorted to Loch Eriboll by frigates of the 9th (Canadian) Escort Group.

The basics of the matter are not in dispute. A group of U-boats had assembled on the announcement of the capitulation of German armed forces, on 8 May, in Narvik, where they awaited developments and further instructions. On the evening of 15 May they headed, as a group and on the surface in accordance with the agreed surrender arrangements, for Trondheim, where they expected to be laid up.

On the following day they were intercepted, along with surface support, supply and tanker vessels, by frigates of the 9th (Canadian) Escort Group. Only at this point does the confusion start. British naval messages transmitted on 16 May initially identified *sixteen* U-boats and five merchant ships bound from Narvik. The instruction was issued that the U-boats were to be escorted to Loch Eriboll and the surface ships were to proceed to Trondheim.

Later on 16 May, in a British naval message, the total number of U-boats in the convoy was amended to *fourteen*, plus three depot ships plus the motor vessels *Stella Polaris* and *Aviso Grille*. And also that day an intercepted German plain-language radio message from the Captain U-Boat Northern Waters to Naval Chief Command Norway Operational Staff stated:

> Captain U-Boats Unit with *Grille, Huascaran, Kamerun, Stella Polaris, Karnten, U-178* [sic], *U-294, U-295, U-312, U-313, U-318, U-363, U-427, U-668, U-716, U-968, U-992, U-997, U-1165* left Narvik at 2000/15th for transfer passage to Trondheim by outer route. Position report every six hours.

So the German naval command themselves identified *fourteen* U-boats (with *U-278* wrongly named as *U-178*) proceeding in convoy southwards from Narvik.

Yet another British naval message on that day, 16 May, repeated the above intercept and confirmed the U-boat identity numbers. At this point it is clear that the suggestion of *fourteen* U-boats comprising the intercepted flotilla was accepted as correct by the officers and men of 9th EG. Commander Layard's recollections set out above constantly refer to this number, and Ron Graham, who was serving at the time aboard HMCS *Nene*, recalls 'We entered the fjord, line ahead, and proceeded up to a bay near the town where we found *fourteen* U-boats and a command ship.'

After tense negotiations described earlier in this narrative it was agreed that the German surface support vessels would proceed to Trondheim and the *fourteen* U-boats would be escorted to Scotland in accordance with the terms of the surrender agreement.

But the following day it became apparent that the U-boats in the group totalled *fifteen*. The five surface ships were despatched to Trondheim and the U-boats began their escorted voyage with 9th EG, on the surface, to Loch Eriboll. Only at this point were the U-boats identified as the original fourteen, plus *U-481*. On Thursday, 17 May a British naval message confirmed that 9th EG had met and was escorting the Vestfjord convoy of *fifteen* U-boats, now including *U-481*

The following day two U-boats from the convoy (*U-312* and one other) were escorted into Lerwick by HMCS *St Pierre* to refuel. They rejoined the convoy and all *fifteen* U-boats arrived in Loch Eriboll on Saturday, 19 May. On the approach to Loch Eriboll, Lt Cdr Franze of *U-278*, who had assumed command of the U-boats on the previous departure of Suhren, issued an unauthorised radio message to each of his fourteen colleagues. This was the 'sour apple' message intercepted at 1730 hours on 18 May by Sam Forsythe, radio operator aboard HMCS *Nene*. The message was headed by the identification numbers of all of the *fifteen* U-boats in the group.

So there we have it. *Fifteen* U-boats left Norway and *fifteen* arrived in Loch Eriboll, the largest joint surrender of Kriegsmarine vessels during the entire course of the war. The confusion over the actual total was due to no more than misinformed radio messages – on both sides – at the commencement of the operation. Understandable, really, for those were hectic times.

U-1305 *is boarded by armed Royal Navy personnel from HMS* Deane *from the British frigate's motor launch on the morning of 10 May 1945. The U-boat flies the black flag of surrender and the commander on the bridge awaits the arrival of the boarding party.* U-1305 *was the second U-boat to surrender in Loch Eriboll, by a few minutes (Imperial War Museum)*

HMS Deane's *motor launch departs* U-1305 *having left aboard a boarding party, guns still trained on the prize, although she now displays the White Ensign below the black flag (Imperial War Museum)*

Above: Seen from the deck of a Royal Navy launch, HMS Deane *escorts* U-1305 *into Loch Eriboll on 10 May 1945 (Imperial War Museum)*

Right: HMS Philante, *the Commander-in-Chief Western Approaches' command yacht, escorts two surrendered U-boats into Loch Eriboll at the start of the mass surrenders in May 1945. This photograph was taken from a circling RAF aircraft and captures the isolated grandeur of the chosen reception location in Scotland's remote far north-west (Imperial War Museum)*

British and German officers and ratings aboard
U-826, *under the White Ensign, await the arrival
of a second surrendered U-boat. The boat's Snorkel
equipment can be seen in some detail and, with
back to camera in the white cap (bottom left),
Kapitanleutnant Olaf Lubke,* U-826's *commander
(Imperial War Museum)*

Taken from the deck of HMS Fitzroy *on 11 May 1945, this
photograph shows* U-826 *alongside* Fitzroy, *displaying the White
Ensign with her German crew accepting the mooring lines from
a second surrendered U-boat – White Ensign also flying – and
supervised by British officers and ratings. The Admiralty caption
identified the second U-boat as* U-236, *but this is incorrect. The
approaching U-boat is* U-293. U-236 *was attacked and damaged
by rocket fire from British Beaufighters on 4 May 1945 whilst on
passage from Kiel to Kristiansand south, and had to be scuttled
later that day. Whiten Head at the entrance to Loch Eriboll is
clearly visible in the background (Imperial War Museum)*

*Royal Navy armed guards look
on as a German submarine
rating carries torpedo firing parts
from* U-826 *to be deposited over
the side (Imperial War Museum)*

Left: German submarine ratings smoking on the deck of their U-boat while others throw petrol jerrycans into the loch – *Official Admiralty caption.* Smoking whilst handling fuel cans was presumably low on the hazard-rating scale after surviving war in a U-boat.
(Imperial War Museum)

Middle: German submarine ratings of *U-826* rescuing one of their crew who fell overboard while discarding ammunition – *Official Admiralty caption*
(Imperial War Museum)

Bottom right: The view astern showing the dismantled 20-mm guns of U-826 under the White Ensign flying from the periscope, with the western shore of Loch Eriboll and the hamlet of Laid in the background (Imperial War Museum)

Bottom left: British sailors scrutinise the stowed Snorkel equipment on the deck of one of the surrendered U-boats in Loch Eriboll – probably U-826. The shot was clearly staged for the benefit of the official Admiralty photographer present on 11 May 1945 (Imperial War Museum)

HMS Rupert *of the 21st Escort Group photographed with a surrendered U-boat alongside – probably taken in Lough Foyle during Operation Deadlight (Author's collection)*

U-516 *photographed from an Allied aircraft on 10 May 1945 after accepting the surrender instructions. The boat is pictured with the black surrender flag flying and crew members crowding the bridge whilst heading for Loch Eriboll and arrest by HMS* Fitzroy *of the 21st Escort Group on 14 May 1945.* U-516 *completed six war patrols and attacked 17 vessels, accounting for 99,000 tons of Allied shipping (Author's collection)*

Left: U-532 *in Liverpool after arrest in Loch Eriboll and escort from there via Loch Alsh. The boat surfaced and surrendered on 10 May between Iceland and the Western Approaches after an extensive trip to the Far East, carrying supplies of wolfram (tungsten), molybdenum, tin, raw rubber and quinine for the German war effort.* U-532 *also had a successful attack career, sinking or damaging 10 ships representing 60,000 tons of Allied shipping. This photograph records Admiral Sir Max Horton's inspection of the boat (Author's collection)*

Right: U-532 *pictured with British crew approaching Barrow-in-Furness docks for unloading after her visit to Liverpool (Author's collection)*

Right: U-255 *in Bergen returning from an active patrol, one of ten undertaken during this boat's career. One warship and eleven merchant ships were sunk, accounting for 55,000 tons of Allied shipping.* U-255*'s commander until June 1943, Kapitanleutnant Reinhard Reche, was the top Arctic U-boat 'Ace' (Author's collection)*

Left: U-255 *with seaplane alongside – a rare shot (Author's collection)*

Right: U-825 *pictured from an Allied aircraft on 10 May 1945 having surfaced and surrendered south-west of the Fastnet light. The boat completed two war patrols from Norwegian waters, sinking two merchant vessels (15,400 tons) and was boarded by a party from HMS* Byron *on 13 May 1945 (Author's collection)*

Above left: U-1231 *photographed in Loch Eriboll showing the White Ensign. When arrested by HMS* Rupert *of the 21st Escort Group on 13 May 1945, the boat was found to be loaded with vast quantities of wine and was suspected of acting as a sort of 'off-licence' to the Kriegsmarine. Arrest came during her second active patrol and she is not credited with any Allied shipping 'kills' (Author's collection)*

Above right: U-2326, *one of the latest Type XXIII 'Elektro' boats, made several attempts to surrender, and seemingly was arrested on each occasion. Here she is shown alongside HMS* Ambrose *off the east coast of Scotland (Author's collection)*

9th (Canadian) Escort Group Operations

Rigth: Three of the frigates of the 9th Escort Group pictured prior to the Norwegian coast and Loch Eriboll events. Left to right: HMCS Loch Alvie (K.428), HMCS Monnow (K.441) and HMCS Nene (K.270) – HMCS Waskesiu (K.330) can be seen on the far left (Author's collection)

Left: Three or four surfaced U-boats approach 9th EG frigates off Trondheim on 17 May 1945 (Dan DeLong/Nene collection)

Right: U-278, the leader of the group of 15 U-boats intercepted off the Norwegian coast on 17 May, photographed from a Royal Naval aircraft approaching Loch Eriboll two days later. The crew crowd the bridge (Imperial War Museum)

Left: Photographed a few minutes later, U-481 leads with a second surrendering U-boat, en route to Loch Eriboll and captivity (Imperial War Museum)

*Photographed from Royal Naval biplane,
U-968 leads another surrendering
U-boat to Loch Eriboll on 19 May 1945
(Imperial War Museum)*

*The leading two of five surrendering
U-boats make for Loch Eriboll on 19
May 1945. This surrender of 15 U-boats,
intercepted in Norwegian waters three
days earlier by the 9th EG, was
the largest such instance
(Imperial War Museum)*

*HMCS Monnow – incorrectly captioned as Loch Alvie – seen escorting a surrendered U-boat from Norway. The
photograph was probably taken underline from HMCS Loch Alvie (Canadian National Archives)*

HMCS Loch Alvie *escorting* U-716 *in Loch Eriboll (Author's collection)*

Above Left: U-992 *comes alongside HMCS* Nene *in Loch Eriboll on the evening of 19 May, with crewmembers preparing to throw a line (Dan DeLong/Nene collection)*

Above right: U-992 *pictured from the deck of HMCS* Nene *in Loch Eriboll, with the crew assembled on the U-boat's bridge (Dan DeLong/Nene collection)*

Right: Crewmembers from HMCS Matane *form a boarding party aboard* U-968 *in Loch Eriboll on 20 May 1945. The starboard side of the Canadian frigate is visible along with the U-boat's emblem on the front of the bridge. The RCN personnel are (left to right): Signalman William Parish; Lt J.J. Coates; and Petty Officer Edwin Massey. U-968 completed eight active patrols, all in Norwegian waters, and was responsible for the destruction of 32,350 tons of Allied shipping – 4 merchant vessels and 2 warships (Canadian National Archives)*

Personal recollections (2)

Eric Williams was present at Loch Eriboll in May 1945, the only official naval reporter to witness and record the surrender of the remnant U-boats. His article was reprinted in *The Scotsman* newspaper on 10 May 2005 and that piece appears below. The reprint formed part of a supplement recording the sixtieth anniversary of the end of the Second World War and was included in a supplement entitled 'The Road to VE Day'.

There are one or two slight errors of fact – only to be expected given the highly charged nature of the occasion – which I have corrected by the use of footnotes. The piece certainly captures the emotion of the occasion and, just a day or two after the capitulation, the entrenched perceptions of two opposing sides. In the circumstances the mutual disrespect is, perhaps, understandable.

I am sincerely grateful to the proprietors of *The Scotsman* for permission to quote this article.

Eric Williams died on 16 February 2009, aged 87.

Eric Williams, Official Naval Reporter, Loch Eriboll, 1945

U-BOAT CREWS SURRENDERED – DEFEATED BUT DEFIANT TO THE LAST

Rising gently on the swell, the motor launch nosed towards the mouth of Loch Eriboll in Scotland's far north-west. It was 10 May 1945. On the crowded bridge anxious eyes scanned seawards, straining to pierce the morning haze, seeking the first sign to mark a long-awaited day of history.

Loch Eriboll had been chosen for the secret rendezvous: a narrow inlet guarded by shaggy brown headlands.

It seemed too good to be true – that the war at sea was finished and the U-boats were defeated. All my colleagues on the bridge were survivors of the U-boat war, including submarine officers.

I had my own score to settle. As a merchant seaman in mid-Atlantic in October 1942, I had been torpedoed while rowing around in a lifeboat, nursing a baby part of the time, before being rescued. Now as an Official Naval Reporter, the only journalist present, I was watching history happen – the formal end of the U-boat war.

From the nearby frigate, HMS *Diane* [sic][1], a sudden blinking of signals tightened the tension. All eyes ranged the swells beyond the loch mouth. There it was! A black blob, then a mast, topped by a faint smoke haze.

Captain M.J. Evans, training captain on the staff of Commander-in-Chief of Western Approaches, in charge of the operation, broke the silence.

'This is the first U-boat I've seen this peace!' he cracked.

As the black hull of the 500-ton *U-1109*[2] slid towards us, our guns trained on her, we wondered: would there be trouble?

The U-boat hove-to, and a whaler was lowered from the frigate carrying an armed guard. As we came alongside, the crew came into focus, and we saw their pallid skins, unkempt beards and grey-green uniforms. So this was the face of the enemy!

There was no Swastika flag. At the mast a green rag of surrender flapped listlessly. I learned later that the ensign had been ditched – But Admiral Doenitz, father of the German fleet, had radioed instructions that it should be saluted before being hauled down. The armed guard leapt aboard, and the Commanding Officer, Oberleutnant von Reisen, from Danzig, offered a lame Nazi salute.

A few seconds later, the White Ensign flew proudly from the conning tower. A Coastal Command flying boat watched overhead as we edged further out into the loch, to deal with the next vessel flying a black flag. As it hove-to, I went with the boarding party. Leaping on to the hull, I nearly lost my footing and scrambled up to the bridge. The commandant, Oberleutnant Helmut Christiansen, of Flensburg, was fair-haired, stocky and sullen. An unhappy man, but obedient. He was following orders. They all did.

Commissioned a few months previously, *U-1305*[3] was on her first patrol. Christiansen proudly claimed success, declaring: 'I know that I have sunk one tramp ship, and I hope I have sunk two destroyers, although I did not see them sinking.'

He spoke fairly good English. When I asked why he had joined the U-boat service, he said stiffly: 'All Germans want to go to the front. I wanted to do it. It was doing more for my country.'

When I asked him whether he was glad the war was over, he stared at me and declared, as though repeating a vow: 'I am glad I helped my country'.

Exactly a year after commissioning, *U-826*[4] was surrendering. She had surfaced after nine weeks submerged using snorkel gear. Her commandant was Kapitanleutnant Lubcke from Potsdam, a professional sailor who had served in cruisers and as a naval aviator. He had a barrel chest and a fiery ginger beard, and was not without humour.

As we stood on the bridge, following a trawler to anchor further down the loch, he recalled: 'When I was at school we used to sing a Scottish song with the words "My heart's in the highlands, my heart is not here!" He shook his head ruefully at the surrounding hills.

First Officer of *U-1305* was 22-year-old Leutnant Edo Schneider, from Hanover, a tall, lean young man who was more talkative. He had been at sea since 1941, and said dejectedly that he would now have no decorations.

I was able to offer but limited sympathy.

'Are you glad the war's over?' I asked.

His mouth tightened: 'We have done our duty to the end,' he insisted.

He was puzzled. 'Do the British hate the Germans?' he asked.

I looked hard at him. 'I have seen newsreels of concentration camps at Belsen and Buchenwald. I have seen terrible things you have done to thousands of people. I have known for years how you have beaten and starved and tortured and killed. How would you feel?'

Immediately he waved my words away. 'You can find atrocities in every country in Europe if you look for them,' he said with a wry smile.

They all took the same line. When I accosted them in turn with the concentration camp atrocities, they dismissed the charge with 'Propaganda!' One even suggested the films were made in Russia, where they were all 'barbarians'.

These men were among the bravest, cleverest and most determined of the enemy, and they fascinated me. What made them tick?

Discipline came first. Unquestioning obedience. They regarded themselves as soldiers obeying instinctively. When I asked one officer whether he would obey an order he knew to be wrong, he smiled deprecatingly. 'We do not get wrong orders,' he said.

Were they all glad the war was over? Kapitanleutnant Helmut Schmoekel from Berlin, commander of *U-802*, the first 750-ton vessel to surrender, replied: 'No – not under these circumstances.'

He had won the Iron Cross First Class for sinking six ships on his first patrol in 1943. Werner Mahnka, a father of four from Hamburg, refused to answer, and turned away with a shrug.

Oberleutnant Frederische Petron (25), of Frankfurt, surrendered *U-516*, his first command, with some resignation and acknowledgement: 'Yes, I am glad the war is over. The world is too unhappy.'

A well-known commandant, 25-year-old Hans-Kurt von Brennen, [sic][5] who had served in U-boats since 1941, was confused. 'What shall we do now?'

I suggested he might help repair some of the thousands of British homes damaged by German bombs.

Nowhere did I find any admission of guilt or regret. Germany had not sought war, I was told. Germany had simply begun the war forced on her by the rest of Europe, following the unjust peace imposed at Versailles after the First World War.

I got to know the commandant of *U-297* [sic][6] best of all.

Kapitanleutnant Leonhard Klingspor was from Zeigen, a small town east of Cologne. He was 27, dark-haired, jaunty-capped with a bold, confident face and forceful, impressive energy. There was a touch of the buccaneer about him.

He smoked cigarettes with a holder, spoke better English than most of his commandant colleagues, and wanted to talk.

From Loch Eriboll all U-boats went to the Kyle of Lochalsh, where I had earlier served on a minelayer. I went down from Eriboll on a destroyer, and I sailed from Lochalsh to Londonderry for the final surrender ceremony on *U-297* [sic][7] spending most of the 24 hours listening to – and arguing with – Klingspor, who claimed he had sunk ten ships, including a Russian destroyer, since 1942. He thought the next war would be between Russia and Britain, considered all concentration camp reports to be 'propaganda – all propaganda!' and made me realise that he and his comrades would simply not believe anything they didn't want to.

It was a pleasant evening, still and warm, as the U-boats ploughed in line astern flanked by British, Canadian, American and French escort vessels.

'Are you a Christian? Do you believe in turning the other cheek?' I asked him. He shook his head. 'I believe in an eye for an eye and a tooth for a tooth,' he said.

'But that's not Christian teaching,' I said. 'That's Old Testament teaching. That's the law of the jungle.'

He smiled and said nothing. We were enjoying a beautiful sunset, for me a bonus to the elation I was feeling now that the war was over and the U-boats were defeated.

Klingspor must have sensed the mood. He gave a cheerful command down the conning tower hatch, and suddenly there was the magic of Mozart. Then Wagner. Then darkness.

About midnight I turned in below, fully dressed. Around three o'clock I was wakened by the roll of the boat and the crash of water coming down the conning tower. Putting on an oilskin, I struggled up to the bridge to find a gale and breaking seas, with *U-293* rolling through 30 degrees or more.

'When I say "Watch Out!" – get down under the bridge,' he instructed.

I nodded confirmation. Then – 'Watch Out!' he called out and the sea smashed over us as we ducked. I saw I was now dependent on the seamanship of a U-boat captain. For security, Klingspor clipped me to a ring on the bridge with a belt attachment. He explained how if he were riding in a following sea chasing up the bridge from astern, he would sit on the bridge, safely chained, and let the waves break under him.

'I like this weather, which is good for attack,' he declared. 'The escorts can do nothing.' He was in his element. He explained how he rode in for the attack. I could not but admire his courage. I felt sick anyhow.

I went below. My trousers had been soaked, and I was wet through. Klingspor gave a command to a nearby rating, who immediately took off his waterproof trousers and gave them to me. I took them as a small fruit of victory, while mine were dried in the engine room.

The gale subsided and, back on the bridge, our conversation resumed. Klingspor talked of his home town, of his army major father, his younger cadet brother, his wife and his two children, whom he had not seen for 15 months.

'Are you a member of the Nazi party?' I inquired.

'No, I am not a member of the party, nor is my father,' he said. 'But that does not matter. A good German is a good Nazi.'

We had an hour before arriving at Londonderry. He motioned me down to the engine room and closed the door. He explained that he was a student of history, and began a long recital of German woes since Bismarck.

As he pursued with passionate emphasis his catalogue of Germany's persecution by the rest of Europe, how Germany had been crowded out, her minorities oppressed, crippled by Versailles, denied a place among the nations, her unity prevented, I realised something of Germany's post-war problems. All Klingspor's comrades had similar convictions.

What would happen now? Kommandant Klingspor's tirade mounted to a triumphant climax. He was obviously well satisfied with his performance – dangerously so, I thought.

Smiling, he leaned over and nudged me. 'See, we'll make you a good Nazi yet!' he declared.

But there was no chance of that as we rounded Culmore Point. We could hear military bands blazing away. There was cheering, and the crowds suddenly broke into Rule Britannia! It was a wonderful moment. I was glad I was in the Royal Navy.

As I left Klingspor, now prepared to step ashore from command to a prison camp, dressed in his No. 1 uniform with Iron Cross First Class and decorations, I told him: 'I am glad you are at last to have the chance of finding out the truth for yourself. You will see how false your propaganda was. Your education is now beginning.'

He looked at me with the trace of a smile. 'I wonder,' he said.

And so did I …

Fifty-one years later, by a remarkable twist of fate, I found out.

In 1995, I wrote an article about him for *The Scotsman*, which found its way to Germany, where it was seen by Klingspor's family.

They were so intrigued that his eldest daughter – a charming woman – came to Britain and visited me to discover more about her father after the surrender.

During an afternoon's earnest discussion, she told me that her father had returned rather bitterly from two years in a prison camp and had immediately resumed as head of the family, which had safely survived as they lived in a substantial house in the country, with a large garden invaluable for growing food.

He had restored the family paper-mill business after a hard struggle. Often they would be visited by former crew members, who were invariably given hospitality and help. He had never involved himself actively in politics, but was a staunch democrat, a devoted father and family man.

Sadly he had been struck down by a brain tumour and had died some seven years previously.

'You might well have become good friends had he lived,' she told me.

We talked about the folly and the tragedy of war, and we toasted frequently over lunch – 'No more war!'

If only this could be true.

---

1   The frigate was HMS *Deane* (K.551)

2   A little mystery here. *U-1109* surrendered in Loch Eriboll on 12 May 1945, the eighth U-boat to do so. *U-1009* was the first vessel to surrender, on 10 May. Oberleutnant Friedrich von Reisen was officer commanding *U-1109*; his opposite number on *U-1009* is not named. Mild confusion or poetic licence?

3   *U-1305* was the second U-boat, by a few minutes, to surrender, on 10 May. Christiansen was commander.

4   *U-826* was the fifth U-boat to surrender, on the afternoon of 10 May 1945.

5   Lt H-K von Bremen was officer commanding *U-764*, which surrendered during the evening of 14 May.

6   This reference should be to *U-293*, the sixth U-boat to surrender, on the morning of 11 May. *U-297* was sunk on
     6 December 1944 by depth charges from frigates HMS *Goodall* and HMS *Loch Insh* eighteen miles ENE of Cape
     Wrath. All hands were lost. Lt Cdr Klingspor commanded *U-293*.

7   See note 6 above.

Local memories

Sadly I conceived the project just a little too late to record the personal memories of Durness locals resident on Loch Eribollside at the time of the surrenders. In February 2009 I did succeed in contacting one or two of the older residents who retained some brief memories of May 1945 and the events unfolding in Loch Eriboll.

Brothers **Walter and John Clarke** at the time lived at Kempie overlooking Loch Eriboll from the eastern side. They each have many memories of growing up through the early 1940s and of the frequent visits of Norwegian whalers to the loch. They recall being taken up the steep hills above Kempie at the time of the U-boat surrenders and seeing set out below them the warships, tugs and armed trawlers spread right across the width of the loch between Ard Neackie and Port-na-con, in constant movement as more U-boats came in to surrender and others were escorted away in small groups.

Michael Mather recalls that during the 1940s his father provided a local mailbus service between Lairg and Durness. Throughout the war there were regular local trips transporting service personnel between the various installations in the immediate area – Army, Navy and Air Force contingents were all stationed in the village – and in the later years of the war there was much activity between Loch Eriboll and Durness. At the time of the U-boat surrenders Michael remembers being driven in his father's bus to Port-na-con to collect Royal Navy personnel needing to be taken into Durness.

He recalls seeing surrendered U-boats in small groups held together on a common anchor off Port-na-con and others moored to British ships in the middle of the loch. British sailors acted as guards on the U-boats, German sailors were aboard but not usually seen, and they never came ashore.

Trawlers go to war

An important but largely unsung element in the U-boat surrender operation was the part played by anti-submarine warfare trawlers (ASWs) in those events. HMTs ('His Majesty's Trawlers') *Harlech Castle* (FY.741), *Grosmont Castle* (FY.671), *Walwyns Castle* (FY.866) and *York City* (FY.110) were despatched to and active off Loch Eriboll on 10 May 1945, and performed essential duties in the first hours of the surrender process under the orders of the Training Captain Western Approaches.

It is incontrovertible that HMT *Harlech Castle* effectively implemented the first arrests of surrendering U-boats in the northern seas when, at 0815 hours on 10 May, she led in *U-1009* and *U-1305* and handed them over to HMS *Byron* of the 21st Escort Group.

Whilst all the records show that the frigate effected the first surrenders it cannot be denied, for there is photographic corroborative evidence, that a prior claim can legitimately be made by anti-submarine warfare trawlers in general and *Harlech Castle* in particular. And these events took place several hours prior to the claimed 'first UK surrender' of *U-249* off Weymouth. But the Senior Service wrote the history, and the trawlers' contributions have been diminished.

Harry Tate's Navy and the Eriboll U-Boat

The Royal Navy Patrol Service was a navy within a navy. Its fighting fleet consisted initially of hundreds of coal-burning trawlers, drifters and whalers brought in from the fishing grounds and dressed for war with ancient guns, most of which had been used to fight the First World War – and some the war before that.

Trawls were replaced by mine-sweeping gear, and Asdic sounding equipment was fitted for anti-submarine patrol. Then off went the fishermen to the bitter waters of the Northern Patrol, to the Channel and 'E-boat alley', to the Atlantic and Arctic convoys, to the U-boat ridden US east coast, Gibraltar and the Mediterranean, Africa, the Indian Ocean and the Far East.

To start with, the ships of the Patrol Service were almost exclusively manned by skippers, mates and men of the Royal Naval Reserve. The crews were fishermen, tugmen and lightermen and their officers were skippers from fishing fleets, with a leavening of senior ranks from the Royal Navy and Royal Naval Reserve to ensure that a modicum of naval discipline was observed.

However, in spite of all the efforts of the naval men in charge and the great influx of newcomers, including Royal Naval Volunteer Reserve officers, the casual, haphazard atmosphere of the fisherman's navy persisted, as did its fiercely stubborn independence, if not downright cussedness. The fleet of rust-stained weather-beaten fishing craft – 'minor war vessels', in the official language of the Admiralty – earned the nickname of 'Harry Tate's Navy', after the renowned 1920s and 30s comedian eternally confounded by modern gadgets and contraptions, the embodiment of the ordinary man struggling with irritations over which he had no control.

Starting with 6,000 men and 600 vessels, 'Harry Tate's Navy' grew to 66,000 men and 6,000 vessels of all descriptions. One very green Ordinary Seaman who joined was a bank clerk named Paul Lund, and his experiences are described in the book *Trawlers Go To War* by Paul Lund and Harry Ludlam (New English Library, England, 1975), from which the following extract is taken, with gratitude and thanks for permission to quote from it here.

> Up on the north coast of Scotland, off Loch Eriboll, Skipper Commander Billy Mullender DSC, was finishing the war as he had begun it, on the bridge of an Asdic trawler. He was steaming *Stella Canopus* [Anti-Submarine-Warfare Trawler HMS *Stella Canopus* (FY.248); Built Cochrane and Sons Shipbuilders Ltd, Selby, Yorkshire; Launched 9 March 1936. Completed April 1936; Taken over by the Admiralty October 1939.] on patrol when suddenly a U-boat surfaced not far off.

Mullender boldly turned to the attack. The trawler's guns were swiftly manned and they had a shell in the breech when, to their skipper's surprise, the U-boat hoisted a black flag of surrender. Mullender steamed alongside and ordered the U-boat commander to hand over his sextant and chronometer. 'But captain,' protested the German commander, 'I am giving you the whole ship!' [The surrendering U-boat was probably *U-802*.]

It was the day of the German surrender and Mullender didn't know it. *Stella Canopus*, however, was cheated of her final glory. Before Mullender could take the U-boat in, an armed yacht with a senior officer on board raced up and took possession of the prize. [This vessel must be HMS *Philante*, HQ vessel of C-in-C Western Approaches, attached to the 21st Escort Group operating from Loch Eriboll at that time.]

Now followed the mass surrenders at sea, and to the trawler *Guardsman* [Military Class Anti-Submarine Warfare Trawler HMS *Guardsman* (T.393); Built Cook, Whelton & Gemmell, Beverley, Yorkshire; Launched 7 June 1944. Commissioned 27 August 1944.], which had been on west coast convoy duty, came a signal honour: she was ordered to the Kyle of Lochalsh to represent Western Approaches trawlers in an escort of the first surrendered U-boats to arrive.

On reaching Lochalsh, *Guardsman* found representative destroyers, sloops, frigates and corvettes already gathered round four U-boats. But, shades of Harry Tate to the last, because of her slower speed, slower even than the U-boats, *Guardsman* was soon left miserably behind and, losing the convoy altogether, turned despondently for Greenock. A little later she did actually escort a big U-boat on a short voyage, and her best moment, representing Asdic trawlers, came when in Wallasey Dock she stood alongside a U-boat placed on view to the people of Liverpool and Birkenhead. [Almost certainly *U-1023*, then on a trip around the west coast of Britain to allow ordinary citizens an experience of a captured German submarine. *U-1023* surrendered at Weymouth on 10 May, was absorbed into the Royal Navy as HM Submarine N.83, and ended her days expended in Operation Deadlight on 8 January 1946.]

Percy Blunden, West Sussex,
Leading Stoker, Submarine Service, Loch Ryan, 1945

I joined the Navy in 1941, and in August 1942 I joined the Submarine Service. After training – mainly on 'H' class submarines, off the west coast of Scotland – then it was off to the Far East in the *Sidon*, sailing on board a wreck of a boat, built in 1926. (In the end we had to leave her tied up between two buoys in Mombasa harbour.)

Then it was off to Trincomalee (Ceylon) where I joined the *Thrasher*, a wonderful boat which I left to come back to the UK in August 1945, on the day after VJ Day. I travelled passage on a cruiser HMS *Enterprise*, and after Foreign Service leave I was drafted to HMS *Sandhurst*, a merchant ship being used as a Submarine Depot ship at Cairn Ryan. This would be about the end of September/ beginning of October 1945.

If ever there was a sight for sore eyes! To see all the U-boats tied up between two buoys, in batches of five, depending on their size.

There was a German maintenance crew on each batch, and the likes of I would go out to oversee them. No trouble was experienced between us – they respected me, as I them – in fact I was regarded as a friend. I still have a picture given me by members of the crew of *U-991*. It is signed by them, and is a gift I really appreciate.

The back of the picture is inscribed with the three signatures of the crewmembers and their ranks and, in German, 'a souvenir of *U-991*'. There is also a small sticker indicating the name of the shop in Berlin that sold the picture. The picture is of the village of Heiligenblut, with the Grossglockner peak in the background. The particular view shown in the picture must have been photographed by countless present-day tourists. But for the crew of the *U-991* it was certainly a reminder of more peaceful days.

As time passed and it came to the starting of the dispersal, I had three trips to Londonderry, Northern Ireland, as crew.

The German submarines were being shared out between each of the Allies, five each to the British, United States, French and Russians. The Germans were not permitted to move them, even in harbour. I must say that the U-boat engines were exceptionally good.

We went out to the U-boats one night in eight. We had to go out on a private yacht to oversee all was well. The crew of the yacht were father and son. They told us that there was no need for us to be on deck, so we could go below and have some sleep! The way that Scotsman handled his yacht to get alongside the U-boats was quite a feat, it was so rough. The west coast of Scotland is not recommended October to January!

When we started sinking the U-boats it was they (the father and son on their yacht) who brought us back to the depot ship. What a job! We British had to steam the U-boats out of Loch Ryan where they were tied up behind destroyers or corvettes, to be sunk off the west coast of Scotland.

On 5th January 1946 I was drafted back to HMS *Dolphin* at Gosport, Hampshire.

Ian Lindsay, Stranraer, Schoolboy, 1945

In May of 1945 I would be ten years old, and I can clearly remember quite a large number of U-boats moored in Loch Ryan. I also recall seeing submarines filmed in a 'Pathe News' newsreel piece at the cinema. It was quite an event locally with all these submarines being there.

I also remember seeing prisoners being marched along Agnew Crescent on their way, probably, to what would be an internment camp just off Sheuchan Street. My clearest recollection is that they marched really well.

Stranraer was a fairly busy place during the war, with airfields at West Freugh and also at Wig Bay, where all the Sunderland and Catalina flying boats were based. There was also an airfield at Castle Kennedy and a large transit camp on the edge of town where thousands of troops passed through.

From the U-boat perspective
Surrenders as seen by the defeated

U-992 – the final days
(An account prepared from notes by Vidar Teigen based on his own researches, and correspondence with Hans Falke).

Having surfaced the previous day, *U-992* arrived in Narvik on 9 May 1945, joined a group of U-boats from the Norway flotillas, and awaited further instructions. The question of the actual date of surrender is problematic; surrender might have taken place on 8 May, at Harstad, or on the 9th, at Narvik. On 16 May they left Narvik in convoy to head for Trondheim, where they expected to be laid up.

On 17 May the U-boats, travelling on the surface in the company of five support vessels, were intercepted by frigates of the 9th (Canadian) Escort Group detached from their duty accompanying convoy JW 67 to Murmansk (the final planned wartime Russian convoy) off the Norwegian coast. The five surface support vessels were instructed to return to Trondheim under the command of FdU Noordmeer Reinhard Suhren (Officer Commanding the U-boats in the Arctic and Barents Sea areas – FdU = Fuhrer der Unterseebootes; FdU Noordmeer = Flag Officer of U-boats in northern waters, including the 13th (Trondheim) Flotilla and the14th (Narvik) Flotilla). The U-boats were escorted to Scotland by the five frigates of the 9th Escort Group.

U-992 arrived in Loch Eriboll on 19 May with the group of arrested U-boats. Once there she was moored alongside HMCS *Nene* together with *U-295*. The latter boat managed to hole the *Nene* whilst manoeuvring, the Canadians making accusations of sloppy seamanship whilst Lt Gunter Wieboldt commanding *U-295* claimed nothing more than a simple accident.

On the evening of 21 May *U-992* was escorted to Loch Alsh by frigates of the 21st Escort Group along with other arrested U-boats, arriving on the 22nd. Non-essential ratings were disembarked for imprisonment and *U-992* sailed the same day to Lisahally, Lough Foyle, Northern Ireland, for impounding. At the time there were at least forty other U-boats tied up in Lisahally.

On 1 September *U-992* sailed for Loch Ryan, on the west coast of the Scottish mainland and a further period of waiting.

Operation Deadlight was agreed on 14 November 1945 under which U-boats were to be towed into the north Atlantic for destruction. The turn of *U-992* came in mid-December 1945. On the 14th she was towed from Loch Ryan by HMS *Fowey* in a group operation led by the Polish destroyer *Piorun*. At the same time *U-739* was taken in tow by the tug *Freedom* with the intention of sinking both boats by the use of torpedoes fired from HM Submarine *Tantivy*. *U-992* and *U-739* were sunk collectively by torpedo action commencing at 1037 hours on 15 December and ending two hours later, during which time *Tantivy*'s Asdic operator heard explosions and breaking-up noises from both targets.

U-992 was one of the Type VIIC ocean-going 'Atlantic' boats which bore the brunt of the convoy battles. She was launched on 24 June 1943 and from the date of her commissioning to her eventual surrender was commanded by Oberleutnant zur See Hans Falke. Oblt Falke previously served aboard *U-46* under Commander Endrass (who had been First Watch Officer under Gunther Prien in the daring October 1939 attack on Scapa Flow which sank HMS *Royal Oak*) at the start of his U-boat service and later aboard *U-118* as Second Watch Officer (2WO) to May 1943.

(According to Falke (and other sources) he was never made First Watch Officer on *U-118*; 1WO Oblt Brammer left the boat for commander training to be replaced by by Oblt Schrotke as 1WO, with Falke continuing as 2WO until he in turn left for commander training in May 1943). Falke was made ObltzS with effect from 1 October 1943. He was awarded the Iron Cross First Class on 10 November 1944 and the German Cross in Gold on 8 February 1945.

Operational patrols for *U-992* involved four brief training and crew familiarisation patrols from Kiel, Stavanger, Bergen and Ramsund between March and June 1944. Active patrols thereafter were:

> 18 June 1944 from Skjomenfjord and return to Narvik 24 July
>
> 29 August from Hammerfest and return 6 September
>
> 12 September from Narvik and return to Hammerfest 3 October
>
> 18 October from Narvik and return 10 November
>
> 30 November from Narvik and return to Bogenbucht 8 December
>
> 16 January 1945 from Bogenbucht and return to Narvik 21 February
>
>> During this patrol *U-992* attacked convoy JW 64 on 13 February, torpedoing and fatally damaging HMS *Denbigh Castle* (K.696) of 1,060 tons.

It is also suggested that on 5 February *U-992* attacked and sank the Soviet 625 ton vessel T-116. T-116 probably survived the attack, but this is difficult to confirm or refute. The Norwegian tanker DT *Norfjell* could also have been hit and damaged, but not sunk. As Vice Admiral B.B. Schofield says in his book *The Arctic Convoys*, '*U-968, U-711* and *U-992* which between them succeeded in torpedoing the tanker *Norfjell* and the freighter *Horace Gray*'. (Macdonald and Jane's, 1977)

17 March from Narvik and return 1 April

1 May from Narvik and return 9 May

ObltzS Hans Falke was interned as a prisoner of war following the surrender of his boat. He was detained in several PoW camps; in Camp No. 17 at Lodge Moor for eleven months, in Camp 184 from 22 August 1946 to 1 May 1947, and finally in Camp 23 for the last days of his captivity. He was released on 19 May 1947.

The following is a most unusual narrative, primarily as it is presented not from the viewpoint of the U-boat Commanding Officer, but rather through the experiences of a member of the crew. And the circumstances by which the account came to be written are also somewhat unusual; these are explained in the notes following the account.

Dissenstion in the ranks

Heinz F.K. Guske, Petty Officer Telegraphist, *U-764*

U-764 left its Flotilla base at Bergen at 2300 on 26 April 1945 under the command of ObltzS von Bremen with orders to proceed to the Pentland Firth, and should there be no targets in that area, to go onwards to the Irish Sea. This would be the boat's seventh operational patrol.

At 0935 on 4 May wireless signals advised that the war would continue and that Norway would be the HQ of operational control. A few hours later a partial surrender in the west was signed. Grossadmiral Doenitz's order for the cessation of U-boat activities was issued by radio at 1614. During the course of the next few days several radio messages were received confirming arrangements for the surrender and for the conduct of U-boats at sea. There were to be no destructions, no scuttlings, no demonstrations and no hostile actions.

In a signal timed at 1200 on 8 May, the British Admiralty announced that the German High Command had been directed to give surrender orders to all U-boats at sea. A radio message timed at 2043 that day and issued in plain language to operational U-boats in the northern sector set out the precise arrangements to be followed with immediate effect. The message was to be repeated at two-hourly intervals. It described the surfacing and signal (black/blue surrender flag) procedures and arrangements to be followed for the destruction of ammunition and the removal of breech blocks and torpedo pistols, the securing of mines and how deck armaments were to be neutralised. Wireless traffic and signal flag communications were to be made in plain language only; the previous instructions as to there being no scuttlings or other damage done to the boats were repeated.

This message was received during the boat's usual daily snorkelling period between 2200 and 2300 that day (8 May). The message was immediately placed before von Bremen, who struck it through and inscribed 'ENEMY PROPAGANDA' across it in blue pencil.

On 9 May the CO called all the officers and NCOs together and, in secrecy from the rest of the crew behind closed doors in the PO's room, proclaimed his intention of ignoring his instructions received in plain language via radio. He would not consider handing over the boat or any of its torpedoes. Since there was insufficient fuel to reach Spain, and since he carried no current charts indicating the minefields in the Kattegat, which precluded a return voyage to Germany, then the boat would jettison all torpedoes and return to Bergen.

If possible the boat would approach submerged and travel as far as possible into the fjord so that the crew could paddle ashore in dinghies after scuttling the boat. If a close approach was not possible due to the presence of enemy forces, then the boat would be scuttled offshore and escape would be as before in dinghies. Thereafter it would be every man for himself. The torpedoes were expended and a course was set for Norway.

But there was a developing resentment amongst the senior crew members. They argued that many were married and all had family responsibilities, the war was over and there was no point in continuing submerged and thereby risking attack as a potentially hostile vessel as it was known that hunter groups were still operating in the northern oceans. A second meeting was held at which the majority view prevailed, notwithstanding the wish of the CO and senior engineering officer to continue to Bergen. The boat's course was reversed.

U-764 surfaced on the morning of 13 May. Radio telegraphist Guske asked permission to transmit the boat's position in plain language in accordance with the surrender instructions already received. Transmissions were being received by the boat from Wick Radio, though the station gave no indication of it in turn receiving signals, on a choice of frequencies, from *U-764*. Guske finally gave up trying, switched off and reported to the CO on the bridge. The CO did not acknowledge this information, and neither did Wick Radio. Guske retired to the lower gun platform aft rail, where he was astonished to find the transmitter aerial disconnected. On the bridge he also found the connection severed. These discoveries made him very suspicious indeed, as the connections could not fail without being physically and intentionally detached – that on the bridge was protected by its own hatch. The reason for Wick Radio not acknowledging the transmissions from *U-764* became all too apparent; they could not have received the transmissions.

Over the next two days there were several contacts by Allied aircraft and surface vessels, and increasingly insistent signals as to why *U-764* had not reported her position as required under the surrender terms. Eventually *U-764* was met by HMS *Fitzroy* and a boarding party completed the surrender process. *U-764* was escorted into Loch Eriboll at 1900 on 14 May.

At 0600 on 15 May *U-764* was escorted to Loch Alsh by HMS *Deane* together with *U-244*. Several conflicting statements were made after the boat's surrender as to the circumstances pertaining on board between 8 May (when the capitulation had been announced) and the 13th (when *U-764*'s presence on the surface became apparent to the Allies) and the delay thereafter in making formal surrender contact. All were either misleading or selectively incomplete, and none mentioned the aborted run towards Norway.

Most of the crew were disembarked on 16 May at Loch Alsh into captivity for the next three years. Essential personnel remained on board to sail the boat across to Lisahally in Northern Ireland, where she remained through the ensuing winter. On 2 January 1946 *U-764* was towed out from Lisahally as an intended torpedo target for the British submarine HMS *Tantivy*. In the event the weather took the upper hand and she had to be despatched by naval gunfire from the Polish destroyer ORP *Piorun*.

Heinz Guske was held as a prisoner of war until 2 March 1948. He did not return to Germany. Commander Hans-Kurt von Bremen was held in a series of camps, among them Camp 184, until his release in 1948.

Heinz F.K. Guske volunteered for Kriegsmarine naval service in order to avoid the inevitability of conscription into the army. He was ordered to report for basic training in January 1940, and on completion of telegraphy and communications instruction was assigned to the fleet tanker *Adria* as his first sea duty.

Between July 1941 and January 1944 he held several communications posts, including duty at the Command Centre U-boat HQ at Kerneval and with the 9th U-Flotilla Communications Centre in Brest. He graduated from Petty Officers' training in June 1943 and joined the crew of *U-764* under Oberleutnant zur See Hans-Kurt von Bremen on 12 January 1944 as Petty Officer Telegraphist. And that is where, it seems, the mutual antipathy started.

ObltzS von Bremen assumed command of *U-764* from the date of her commissioning in May 1943. On Guske's reporting for duty in January the following year he saluted his commander and stood to attention. Commanding Officer von Bremen, apparently, ignored the new arrival and did not return the salute, 'either then or subsequently'. It was not the best of starts.

For the next sixteen months, through six operational patrols, Guske became increasingly convinced of von Bremen's inept command of the boat. Guske's view of matters includes accusations of arrogance, superciliousness, sloppy log-keeping, falsehood, fabrication, omission, concealment, refusal to attack, gross incompetence and stupidity, arrogant insubordination, shifting blame from himself to his crew (for whom he had 'little or no regard') and even, immediately prior to surrender, collusion in the sabotage of his boat's radio transmission equipment. He 'demanded absolute obedience and prompt execution of his orders [...] whereas he ignored the orders and directives of his superiors at U-boat HQ whenever it served his own purpose'. Quite a catalogue of accusations.

Guske makes the point that every U-boat was obliged to transmit to HQ regular signals giving relevant data of the boat's progress and actions. He also emphasises that the commander was in sole charge of these Kriegstagebuchen (KTB, or War Diaries) transmissions and that he determined, solely, the content, and therefore what was included or omitted. But Guske, as telegraphist, was aware of what was contained in these signals and became increasingly convinced of their inaccuracy and irrelevance.

The matter came to a head after the passage of forty years from the date of these events. In 1985 Guske discovered that von Bremen had written a book describing the service history of *U-764*, based on the KTBs, and had distributed copies to surviving crew members. Since Guske had remained in the UK after his release from prisoner-of-war captivity and had had no contact with his former colleagues thereafter, he assumed that von Bremen must have felt safe from exposure or contradiction.

It must therefore have come as something of a shock to von Bremen when he realised that his former telegraphist (one of very few crew members aware of the wildly inaccurate KTBs) was alive and well and living in England. He subsequently refused all contact with Guske, as did Egbert Kandler (former second watch officer aboard *U-764* and von Bremen's uncritical supporter), and so Guske determined that his only recourse was to publish his own book setting out the facts as he saw them. *The War Diaries of U-764: Fact or Fiction* was published in the USA in 1992, and forms the basis of the foregoing narrative.

I am unaware of any reaction by von Bremen to the publication of Guske's book and its very pointed and serious accusations. I suspect that it was met with an embarrassed silence. The entire saga is unsatisfactory from a researcher's viewpoint. Post-war research has relied heavily on KTB content, which should be regarded as reliable. Unimpeachable the KTBs of *U-764* might be, but that does not necessarily guarantee their veracity.

The commander's debriefing

Oberleutnant Karl Jobst, Commander *U-2326*, May 1945

Left Stavanger on the 4 May at 0100 and was again escorted as far as Sveiname. Then dived to 50 metres and went across the North Sea and the English minefield just north of Aberdeen. In order to charge batteries we snorkelled every day between 2300 and approximately 0330. We also ventilated the boat for 10–15 minutes between 1200 and 1400. Just about half way from Aberdeen to Peterhead we altered course to the southward on the British convoy course. That was about midday on the 7th.

It had been impossible until then to fix our position as the weather had been drizzly and soundings did not give an accurate fix. On the 8th we were abreast of May Island. The clouds broke for a short while and the Island was quite clearly visible. At midday I was run over by two destroyers which were coming from the east en route up the Firth of Forth. The boat was not detected. During the night of 8/9 May we bottomed in 60 metres near May Island.

In the forenoon of the 9th we heard noises of ships' screws on the hydrophones. We came off the bottom and proceeded in the direction of the noise. Through the periscope I saw that a corvette and a frigate had already passed over me. Inclination was very great (160–180). About five minutes later a small escort ship passed along my port side about 200 metres away. This was too short a range at which to fire so I did not attack. Astern of the convoy – a tanker of 1,500 tons and a small coaster of 500–800 tons – were two more frigates. One of them turned towards me. I dived to 40 metres and made off southwards towards St Abb's Head. In the evening at 2200 I surfaced, both to charge the batteries and to try to get W/T reception.

As I had heard no depth charge explosions, nor W/T messages, I decided to go north to Aberdeen and then eastwards into the North Sea. I hoped to hear W/T messages as I approached Norway. On the morning of 10 May at 0100 I heard the news by Norwegian Radio that Germany had capitulated. At 0230 I passed a big convoy coming from the north but as I was not sure whether the Norwegian station had spoken the truth or not, I did not attack the convoy. Our position was then between the convoy course and the English minefield. At this time the batteries were fully charged.

I altered course to the northward. At about 0430 we sighted a 10,000 ton tanker which was being escorted northwards by a frigate. I had still had no orders by W/T. The frigate attacked me and I crash-dived when she was 300 metres away. No depth charges were dropped. At about 1430 I was on the surface between Aberdeen and Peterhead. I then went eastwards through the minefield.

On 11 May I surfaced in order to wait for orders from Operations. The English station gave us news of our surrender and said that German submarines in our area were to make for German ports. In Kiel they said the British Admiral's flag was flying. As I was already far into the North Sea and only knew the position of the minefields in the northern part of the North Sea near the Skagerrak and Kattegat I decided to make for Kiel. On the evening of the 11th and the morning of the 12th we had our first complete W/T instructions. On the 10th we had heard that all W/T transmissions were to cease. I had a black flag placed next to our ensign and told the crew of the instructions in the signal. The transmission of my PCS was not heard by the British Station.

At 0700 on the 12th a Liberator flew over us and demanded my number. This I gave and again proceeded. Further flashing was very difficult for we could only read part of what was sent. The Liberator flew very low over us, circled and then dropped a bomb. After about two minutes I was ordered to steer 270. I turned to this and proceeded at best speed. This aircraft was later relieved by another. By this time the British Station GZZ had heard our PCS and told us to make for Loch Eriboll. The last we heard from the aircraft was 'See you in Dundee'. From this I took it that I should go to Dundee.

During the night of 12 and 13 May we had no aircraft escort. I went westwards on the surface. On the morning of the 12th the destroyer HMS *Vivien* (L.33) came to meet me. I told him my number and my intention of steering for Dundee. I was told to go to Edinburgh.

On the afternoon of the 13th I sighted the defence vessel at one end of the minefield, and as I did not know my position I went straight up to him and said 'I have orders to go to Edinburgh and wish to know my position'. I was told to steer a westerly course. At the same time along came an RAF rescue launch, and told us to follow him to Dundee. I took up station astern of the launch.

On 14 May I waited in the proximity of Bell Rock for further instructions. The launch returned at 0500 and took me into Dundee where I secured alongside the King George Wharf. The boat was searched and all firearms removed. All secret code books etc. were given up and scuttling charges handed over.

On the morning of the 16th we left Dundee to fire our Type T IIIA torpedoes near the minefield. This was done under the supervision of the Commanding Officer of British submarine HMS *Ultimatum* (P.34). At 1900 we left for Loch Eriboll with two officers, one PO and a signalman from P.34 on board. We were escorted by a frigate and made fast alongside another in Loch Eriboll on the morning of the 18th. In the afternoon the boat was visited by the Senior British Officer present.

Escorted by a frigate we left for Loch Alsh and on the 19th HMS *Kempthorne* (K.483) escorted us to Londonderry.

General Remarks:

The W/T communications were very bad in both operations. Submerged, using the Snorkel aerial, and on the surface using both main and auxiliary aerials it was almost impossible to receive anything. Neither long nor short waves could at any time be received over the D/F aerial. Pressure when using the Snorkel varied from 250 to 280 millibars. This had no adverse effect on the crews' ears, but it was very damp. The Commanding Officer and 1st Lieutenant were fully cross-examined by Captain Keay in Dundee.

Signed Karl Jobst

Ob.Lt.zs.u.Kmqt.

U.2326

The foregoing is the quick initial translation of the Operational Report from the Commanding Officer of *U-2326* covering the period 4 to 20 May 1945. One or two spelling and grammar errors have been corrected, in the interests of clarity, and paragraph breaks have been inserted in order to make what was originally a solid body of text easier on the eye. The facts and the context have in no way been altered.

U-2326 was one of the latest Type XXIII 'Elektro' boats built as smaller versions of the Type XXI, and as such was of very great interest to the Allies after the end of the war. The boat had been in service for rather less than a year (commissioned 10 August 1944) at the time of her surrender and arrest. Oberleutnant zur See Karl Jobst assumed command at her commissioning, having previously served as first watch officer aboard *U-744* between April 1943 and February 1944.

U-2326 was attached to the 11th U-boat Flotilla (Bergen) operating from Stavanger, Norway from February 1945, her service prior to that being taken up with sea-trialling and training, with 4th Flotilla (Stettin) and 32nd Flotilla (Konigsberg) to January 1945. She undertook three non-operational patrols: 30 March from Kiel returning to Larvik on 3 April, 5 April from Larvik returning to Kristiansand on 6 April, and 9 April Kristiansand returning to Stavanger on 11 April 1945, and completed one active patrol, leaving Stavanger on 19 April 1945. That patrol took her into the North Sea off Britain's east coast, around St Abb's Head. She returned to base on 27 April. On 3 May she put to sea for her second (uncompleted) operational patrol, which ended with her surrender on 14 May as described by her commanding officer above. She neither sank nor attacked any Allied vessels during her active career.

ObltzS Karl Jobst was interned as a prisoner of war in Camp 9 following the arrest of the boat.

As *U-2326* was an example of the latest development by the Kriegsmarine of the U-boat designed principally for continuous operation under water, the Allied navies took a particular interest in her and she was excluded from Operation Deadlight. She was extensively evaluated and trialled by the British Navy in 1945/46, acquiring the redesignation N-35 during that period. Later in 1946 she was transferred to the French navy, and ended her days in a fatal diving accident off Toulon on 6 December 1946.

U-BOATS ESCORTED TO LOCH ERIBOLL
Types, specifications and capabilities

In the decade from 1935 very many U-boat types were developed or planned. In round figures twenty-two different types were actually built and deployed as sea-going attack vessels, with two more built as experimental types. And a further thirty-one design projects were either still-born on the drawing board or commenced in the shipyard but not completed by the end of hostilities.

The first true submarines – vessels designed to operate principally under water – were Types XXI and XXIII, and an example of the latter was berthed in Loch Eriboll prior to escort to Loch Alsh. All other classes should more correctly be termed 'submersibles' – vessels which could operate under water for varying periods but which were designed to spend much of their operational time on the surface. But 'submarine' has become a generic term in common use understood by all to refer to any vessel capable of being intentionally submerged and surfaced at will.

The Type VIIC U-boat (sometimes referred to as the 'Atlantic boat') was the main player in convoy battles; the Type IX was deployed in distant waters and carried the U-boat campaign far away from the European theatre. Examples of each type were berthed in Loch Eriboll.

The differing types or sub-types of U-boats temporarily berthed in Loch Eriboll in May 1945 on their way to the west coast and onwards were:

Type VIIC & VIIC/41

Built as ocean-going submarines with single hulls and saddle tanks, six water-tight compartments and a diving depth of 100 to 200 metres. Armed with five 21 inch torpedo tubes (four forward and one aft), fourteen torpedoes or up to 39 mines and guns of 20 mm and 88 mm, the Type VIIC had a complement of 4 officers and between 40 and 56 ratings, depending on specification.

Dimensions were 66.5 metres long by 6.2 metres beam by 4.74 metres keel to conning tower and displacing 769 tons surfaced or 871 tons submerged it could attain speeds of almost 18 knots surfaced or almost 8 knots submerged. It had a range of 8,500 miles at 10 knots surfaced or 80 miles at 4 knots submerged.

Type IXC & IXC/40

Designed as a long-range ocean-going submarine the Type IX, a development of the Type IA, had a double hull, five water-tight compartments and a diving depth of 100 to 200 metres. Armed with six 21 inch torpedo tubes (four forward and two aft), 22 torpedoes or up to 66 mines, a 105 mm gun and 37 mm and 20 mm anti-aircraft guns. From 1943 the105 mm gun was replaced by two twin 20 mm guns fitted to the rear of the bridge in place of the single 20 mm gun. The complement was 4 officers and 42 ratings.

Dimensions were (Type IXC/40 in brackets) 76.7 m x 6.76 m x 4.7 m (76.7 m x 6.86 m x 4.67 m) displacing 1,120 tons or 1,232 tons submerged (1,144 tons/1247 tons). Both variants attained speeds of 18 knots surfaced and almost 8 knots submerged and had ranges of 13,450 miles at 10 knots surfaced or 64 miles at 4 knots submerged (13,850 or 63 miles respectively).

Type XXI (not represented in Loch Eriboll)

The Type XXI, designed with a very streamlined shape, high submerged speed and for operation with a 'Snort,' was the first true submarine, as distinct from a submersible, boat. It had a double hull with seven water-tight compartments and a diving depth of 120 to 240 metres. The build process, for the first time, involved construction in eight prefabricated sections.

It displaced 1,621 tons surfaced or 1,819 tons submerged, achieved a surfaced speed of 15 knots but almost 18 knots submerged and could attain 3.5 knots when 'silent running'. Its range was15,500 miles at 10 knots surfaced or 110 at 10 knots submerged. The Type XXI boats became known as 'Elektro' boats because of the number and power of the new super-light high-capacity batteries which enhanced their submerged capabilities.

Armament was six 21 inch torpedo tubes forward with 23 torpedoes (or 14 torpedoes with 12 mines) and four 20 mm anti-aircraft guns. Designed to operate for up to three days submerged at 4 knots without having to recharge or ventilate, accommodating a complement of 5 officers and 52 ratings.

The XXI boats could locate the enemy by radar or hydrophone at depth and attack at speed, assess the target range and bearing by sonar and hydrophone, attack without the use of periscope and escape undetected, again at high speed, as Allied sonar was ineffective against submerged submarines travelling in excess of 12 knots. That Allied shipping losses were not so much greater was due to the long training period necessary in this very technically advanced U-boat, which delayed their operational deployment.

Type XXIII

Designed for use in Mediterranean and coastal waters the Type XXIII was the little brother of the Type XXI. It had a single hull, three water-tight compartments and could dive to between 100 and 200 metres. It was constructed in four prefabricated compartments, displaced 232 tons surfaced or 258 tons submerged and could achieve almost 10 knots surfaced and more than 12 knots submerged (3.5 knots when 'silent running'). The type was simply armed with two 21 inch torpedo tubes and two torpedoes. The complement was 2 officers and 12 ratings.

U-boat insignia and emblems

Distinctive insignia were popularly sported by the majority of U-boat crews throughout the war. Emblems and insignia were expressions of individuality; they could also sometimes represent a unique feature or meaning connected with their boat.

Propaganda and superstition also doubtless influenced the form the talismans took. After all, combatants spending their active life submerged and often under attack needed all the luck they could get. It comes as no surprise therefore that depictions of clover for good fortune or cupid for accurate aiming featured prominently throughout the range of emblems selected.

One of the better-known emblems was the golden horseshoe sported by Otto Kretschmer, perhaps the foremost U-boat ace of the Second World War. He chose to display his good-luck charm inverted, with the gap at the base, whereas the usual form in British usage was with the gap at the top, 'so the luck could not run out'. On 17 March 1941 Kretschmer's luck ran out. His boat U-99 sank after depth-charging by HMS *Walker* when south-east of Iceland. The successful destroyer also displayed a good-luck horseshoe, but in the U format. Kretschmer spent the next six and a half years in captivity as a prisoner of war.

Prior to the outbreak of the Second World War U-boats tended to have their individual numerals painted prominently in large white characters perhaps 1.5 metres tall on the conning tower. In wartime these identifying markings were discontinued, with U-boats adopting an overall neutral grey in order to keep the enemy guessing about the deployment of undersea forces. But it was not long before U-boat crews began to adopt insignia and emblems as a means of expressing their individualism.

In addition to individual U-boat emblems, each graduating class from U-boat academy might also choose their own emblem. The crew of 1936 chose Olympic Rings, recognising the international games held that year in Munich. An upright dagger piercing a wedding ring was chose for 1937, the pictorial interpretation being 'Win first, then marry'. And entire U-boat flotillas displayed emblems. The 7th U-Flotilla adopted the snorting bull after that displayed on Gunther Prien's celebrated *U-47*, which penetrated the protection of Scapa Flow on 14 October 1939 under his command and sank HMS *Royal Oak*, pride of the British navy; the 9th U-Flotilla had the laughing swordfish as its talisman.

But not all boats had emblems, and many had more than one. For example, a boat could display its flotilla emblem, the graduating class emblem and the boat's individual emblem. Very often when a new captain took command of the boat he would simply add his own emblem to those displayed, rather than risk compromising the good fortune which the boat had already accumulated. Individual U-boat insignia were also worn on uniforms, sewn onto caps and even imprinted on the crews' personal items.

With the advent of the true submarines – Types XXI and XXIII – designed to spend most of their time submerged, the tradition of displaying multiple emblems on each vessel gradually diminished, though it did not entirely vanish by the end of the War. There is photographic evidence of at least one U-boat (*U-968*) proudly displaying its individual emblem after surrender in Loch Eriboll.

In the individual histories and fates of the Loch Eriboll U-boats which follow, relevant insignia and emblems are depicted with each entry, where known and recorded. In very few cases no emblem is shown and in these instances the likelihood is that the boat displayed none. Of the approximately 1,100 U-boats which saw combat service between 1939 and 1945, 900 or so are recorded as displaying a unique or a common flotilla emblem. It was very much the exception, therefore, for a U-boat not to display an outward characterisation of its individuality.

The detailed U-boat descriptions which follow are divided into two sections.

Section one gives individualised data on each of those thirty-three U-boats which were, incontrovertibly, escorted into and berthed in Loch Eriboll, by the 9th and 21st Escort Groups, for disarming and onward delivery between 10 May and 21 May 1945.

Section two gives similar data for the six additional U-boats about which there linger some suggestions, of varying strength, that they might have made brief appearances in Loch Eriboll whilst being escorted from Germany or Norway to Loch Ryan or Lough Foyle or from there back to the east coast.

Whilst the official record does not entertain the possibility of these additional vessels having visited Loch Eriboll, I feel that in the interests of setting out a comprehensive survey of all likely candidates, their details should be recorded. For example, the written service history of one His Majesty's warships, HMS *Loch Eck* (K.422), includes a clear specific reference to that vessel escorting an identified U-boat to Loch Eriboll; that evidence ought not to be dismissed as unreliable out of hand, though perhaps the later contradictory War Diary references might be regarded as conclusive. And mention must be made of the Dutch-built *UD-5/O-27* boat. British and Dutch records confirm her passage from Norway to Northern

Ireland via Scapa (the original intention had been for the boat to be received into Loch Eriboll on the way) and her identification in and return from Lisahally by a Dutch recovery crew. Her well-worn state at the capitulation could mitigate in favour of a brief stopover in Loch Eriboll on her return passage from Northern Ireland to Dundee, where she was partially refitted prior to her return to the Netherlands. These are just two examples of the difficulties researchers encounter when attempting to set out a definitive record.

Recent intensive research amongst the preserved contemporary documentation has, I am now prepared to accept (in the majority of cases), effectively settled the outstanding questions relating to the six 'possible' additional Loch Eriboll U-boats. Their relevant details are set out here so that future researchers might not spend time and effort pursuing an irrelevant goal. It is a shame to make the 'possibles' 'improbables' then, but it all adds to an already fascinating subject.

And, finally, an explanatory note regarding the arrival and departure times of each surrendered U-boat at Loch Eriboll, and its subsequent arrival time at Loch Alsh. Pat Godwin's narrative 'The Forgotten Operation' included in Personal Recollections (1) gives these details for most of the thirty-three surrendered U-boats processed in Loch Eriboll between 10 and 21 May. But of course a separate detailed record was maintained aboard HMS *Philante* by Acting Captain M.J. Evans standing in for Admiral Max Horton. Inevitably there are discrepancies between the two records. I have favoured, perhaps irrationally, the Evans compilation as likely to be the more reliable, and data from that source is quoted in the individual U-boat information following.

Section one

U-244

Type   VIIC
Ordered   10 April 1941
Yard   Germania Werft, Kiel
Job No.   678
Keel laid   24 October 1942
Launched   2 September 1943
Commissioned   9 October 1943

Circumstances of capture

Surfaced and surrendered on 12 May 1945 south-west of the Fastnet Light, Eire.
Per Pat Godwin, crew member of HMS *Fitzroy*, U-244 surrendered to HMS *Deane* of the 21st Escort Group. Escorted into Loch Eriboll at 1830 hours on 14 May 1945.

History after capture, and fate

U-244 was escorted from Loch Eriboll at 0600 hours on 15 May, still carrying ten torpedoes, and delivered to Loch Alsh by HMS *Deane*. Arrival was recorded as 1600 hours on that day.

Towed out from Lisahally on 29 December 1945 by the tug *Enchanter* for destruction under Operation Deadlight. En route to the final disposal point the tow parted and *U-244* was sunk by gunfire from the Polish destroyer ORP *Piorun* at 5546N x 0832W later that day.

U-255

Type   VIIC
Ordered   23 September 1939
Yard   Bremer Vulkan, Bremen–Vegesack
Job No.   20
Keel laid   21 December 1940
Launched   8 October 1940
Commissioned   29 November 1941

Circumstances of capture

U-255 was one of the most successful Arctic boats. On its first operational cruise, in July 1942, the boat was the first to locate the ill-fated convoy PQ 17, from which it sank four ships. During its later career it sank a further eight Allied vessels and damaged another. *U-255* was severely damaged by air attack in August 1944 and decommissioned at St Nazaire. Although isolated, the base remained in German hands.

   U-255 sailed from St Nazaire, France on 8 May 1945 for Norway but surfaced en route to surrender west of Fastnet Light, Eire. Per Pat Godwin, crew member of HMS *Fitzroy*, this U-boat surrendered to HMS *Byron* of the 21st Escort Group. Escorted into Loch Eriboll at 0730 hours on 17 May 1945.

History after capture, and fate

U-255 was escorted from Loch Eriboll at 1300 hours on 17 May and delivered to Loch Alsh by HMS *Byron*, arriving at 2130 that day.

   Towed out from Loch Ryan on 11 December 1945 by HMS *Cubitt* (K.512) for destruction under Operation Deadlight and sunk as an aircraft target by rockets fired from a Beaufort of 254 Squadron RAF at 5116N x 1338W on 13 December 1945.

U-278

Type   VIIC
Ordered   10 April 1941
Yard   Bremer Vulkan, Bremen-Vegesack
Job No.   43
Keel laid   26 March 1942
Launched   2 December 1942
Commissioned   16 January 1943

Circumstances of capture

U-278 surrendered on 8 May 1945 in Norwegian waters and was one of the group of fifteen U-boats intercepted on 16 May when on passage from Vestfjord to Trondheim by the 9th Escort Group. *U-278* was commanded by Lt Cdr Franze, who assumed command of the entire group of fifteen on the departure of FdU Nordmeer Suhren on 16 May. The group arrived in Loch Eriboll at 2000 hours on 19 May. *U-278* was boarded by a party from HMS *Philante*.

History after capture, and fate

U-278 was escorted from Loch Eriboll at 2000 hours on 21 May to Loch Alsh, where she arrived at 0900 hours on 22 May.

   Towed out from Lisahally on 31 December 1945 by HMS *Cawsand Bay* (K.694) for destruction under Operation Deadlight. En route to the final disposal point the tow parted and *U-278* was sunk by gunfire from Polish destroyer ORP *Blyskawica* at 5544N x 0821W later that day.

U-293

Type   VIIC/41
Ordered   14 October 1941
Yard   Bremer Vulkan, Bremen–Vegesack
Job No   58
Keel laid   17 November 1942
Launched   30 July 1943
Commissioned   8 September 1943

Circumstances of capture

Surfaced 10 May 1945 off the Hebrides, approximately 50 miles north of St Kilda, and circled by Liberators of 59 Squadron operating from Ballykelly, Northern Ireland. Per Pat Godwin, crew member of HMS *Fitzroy*, this U boat surrendered to HMS *Fitzroy* of the 21st Escort Group. Escorted into Loch Eriboll at 0900 hours on 11 May.

History after capture, and fate

U-293 was escorted from Loch Eriboll at 1300 hours on 11 May and delivered to Loch Alsh by HMS *Fitzroy* at 2015 hours that same day.

Towed out from Loch Ryan on 11 December 1945 by the tug *Masterful* for destruction under Operation Deadlight. Used as an aircraft target on 13 December 1945 and sunk by gunfire from HMS *Orwell* (G.59) later that day after sustaining serious aircraft damage.

U-294

Type   VIIC/41
Ordered   14 October 1941
Yard   Bremer Vulkan, Bremen–Vegesack
Job No.   59
Keel laid   22 December 1942
Launched   27 August 1943
Commissioned   4 October 1943

Circumstances of capture

U-294 surrendered on 8 May 1945 in Norwegian waters and was one of the group of fifteen boats intercepted on 16 May when on passage from Vestfjord to Trondheim by the 9th (Canadian) Escort Group. The group arrived in Loch Eriboll on 19 May at 2000 hours. *U-294* was boarded by a party from HMCS *Loch Alvie* of the 9th (Canadian) Escort Group.

History after capture, and fate

U-294 was escorted from Loch Eriboll to Loch Alsh by ships of the 9th Escort Group at 2020 hours on 20 May, arriving there at 0730 hours the following day.

Towed out from Lisahally on 29 December 1945 by HMS *Loch Shin* (K.421) for destruction under Operation Deadlight. The tow parted and *U-294* was returned to Moville by the tug *Saucy*. On 30 December *U-294* was again towed out for destruction by HMS *Loch Shin* and sunk by gunfire from HMS *Offa* (G.29) at 5544N x 0840W the following day.

U-295

Type   VIIC/41
Ordered   14 October 1941
Yard   Bremer Vulkan, Bremen–Vegesack
Job No.   60
Keel laid   31 December 1942
Launched   13 September 1943
Commissioned   20 October 1943

Circumstances of capture

U-295 surrendered on 8 May 1945 in Norwegian waters and was one of the group of fifteen U-boats intercepted on 16 May when on passage from Vestfjord to Trondheim by the 9th (Canadian) Escort group. The group arrived in Loch Eriboll at 2000 hours on 19 May. *U-295* was boarded by a skeleton guard party from HMS *Fitzroy* of the 21st Escort Group.

History after capture, and fate

U-295 was escorted from Loch Eriboll at 2000 hours on the 21 May to Loch Alsh, where she arrived at 0900 hours the following day.

Towed out from Loch Ryan on 15 December 1945 for destruction under Operation Deadlight by HMS *Pytchley* (L.92). The weather was too rough for the intended destruction by submarine torpedo fire from HMS *Tantivy* (P.319) to be carried out, and *U-295* was sunk by gunfire from Polish destroyer ORP *Blyskawica* at 5614N x 1037W on 17 December 1945.

U-312

Type   VIIC
Ordered   5 June 1941
Yard   Flender-Werke, Lubeck
Job No.   312
Keel laid   10 April 1942
Launched   27 February 1943
Commissioned   21 April 1943

Circumstances of capture

U-312 surrendered on 8 May 1945 in Norwegian waters and was one of the group of fifteen U-boats intercepted on 16 May when on passage from Vestfjord to Trondheim by the 9th (Canadian) Escort Group. The group arrived in Loch Eriboll at 2000 hours on 19 May. *U-312* was boarded by a party from HMS *Rupert* of the 21st Escort Group.

History after capture, and fate

U-312 was escorted from Loch Eriboll to Loch Alsh by HMS *Deane* at 2000 hours on 21 May, arriving at 0900 hours the following day.

Towed out from Lisahally on 28 November 1945 for destruction under Operation Deadlight by HMS *Cubitt* (K.512) as an aircraft bombing target. *U-312* foundered and sank whilst under tow on 29 November at 5535N x 0754W.

U-313

Type   VIIC
Ordered   25 August 1941
Yard   Flender-Werke, Lubeck
Job No.   313
Keel laid   11 May 1942
Launched   27 March 1943
Commissioned   20 May 1943

Circumstances of capture

U-313 surrendered on 8 May 1945 in Norwegian waters and was one of the group of fifteen U-boats intercepted on 16 May when on passage from Vestfjord to Trondheim by the 9th (Canadian) Escort Group. The group arrived in Loch Eriboll at 2000 on 19 May. U-313 was boarded by a party from HMS *Fitzroy* of the 21st Escort Group.

History after capture, and fate

U-313 was escorted from Loch Eriboll to Loch Alsh at 2000 hours on 21 May 1945 by HMS *Fitzroy*, arriving at 0900 hours the following day.

Towed out from Loch Ryan on 20 December 1945 by HMS *Blencathra* (L.24) for destruction under Operation Deadlight. U-313 foundered in 55 fathoms on 21 December 1945 at 5540N x 0824W.

U-318

Type   VIIC/41
Ordered   14 October 1941
Yard   Flender-Werke, Lubeck
Job No.   318
Keel laid   14 October 1942
Launched   25 September 1943
Commissioned   13 November 1943

Circumstances of capture

U-318 surrendered on 8 May 1945 in Norwegian waters and was one of the group of fifteen U-boats intercepted on 16 May when on passage from Vestfjord to Trondheim by the 9th (Canadian) Escort Group. The group arrived in Loch Eriboll at 2000 hours on 19 May. U-318 was boarded by a skeleton guard party from HMS *Conn* of the 21st Escort Group.

History after capture, and fate

U-318 was escorted from Loch Eriboll at 2000 hours on 21 May to Loch Alsh, where she arrived at 0900 hours the following day.

Towed out from Loch Ryan on 20 December 1945. The tow parted the following day and U-318 was sunk by gunfire from Polish destroyer ORP *PioRun* at 5547N x 0830W.

U-363

Type   VIIC
Ordered   20 January 1941
Yard   Flensburger Schiffsbau
Job No.   482
Keel laid   23 December 1941
Launched   17 December 1942
Commissioned   18 March 1943

Circumstances of capture

U-363 surrendered on 8 May in Norwegian waters and was one of the group of fifteen U-boats intercepted on 16 May when on passage from Vestfjord to Trondheim by the 9th (Canadian) Escort Group. The group arrived in Loch Eriboll at 2000 hours on 19 May. *U-363* was boarded by a party from HMS *Deane* of the 21st Escort Group.

History after capture, and fate

U-363 was escorted from Loch Eriboll at 2000 hours to Loch Alsh by HMS *Rupert* on 21 May, arriving at 0900 hours the following day.

Towed out from Lisahally on 31 December 1945 by the tug *Saucy* for destruction under Operation Deadlight. En route to the final disposal point the tow parted and *U-363* was sunk by gunfire from Polish destroyer ORP *Blyskawica* at 5545N x 0818W that day.

U-427

Type   VIIC
Ordered   5 June 1941
Yard   Danziger Werft, Danzig
Job No.   128
Keel laid   27 July 1942
Launched   6 February 1943
Commissioned   2 June 1943

Circumstances of capture

U-427 surrendered on 8 May 1945 in Norwegian waters and was one of the group of fifteen U-boats intercepted on 16 May when on passage from Vestfjord to Trondheim by the 9th (Canadian) Escort Group. The group arrived in Loch Eriboll at 2000 hours on 19 May. *U-427* was boarded by a party from HMS *Conn* of the 21st Escort Group.

History after capture, and fate

HMS *Caistor Castle* (K.690) is mentioned in some records as having escorted *U-427* from Loch Eriboll to Loch Alsh, though I have found no other mention of this frigate being present in Loch Eriboll. The escort to Loch Alsh commenced at 2000 hours on 21 May and arrived at 0900 hours the following day.

Towed out from Loch Ryan on 20 December 1945 by the tug *Enchanter* for destruction under Operation Deadlight. *U-427* was one of the few U-boats to be successfully towed to the selected disposal point; she was sunk by gunfire at 5604N x 0935W on 21 December 1945 in over 500 fathoms. British warships HMS *Onslaught* (G.04), HMS *Zetland* (L.59), and HMS *Fowey* (L.15) and Polish destroyer ORP *PioRun* all took part.

U-481

Type   VIIC
Ordered   5 June 1941
Yard   Deutsche Werke, Kiel
Job No.   316
Keel laid   6 February 1943
Launched   25 September 1943
Commissioned   10 November 1943

Circumstances of capture

U-481 surrendered on 8 May 1945 in Norwegian waters and was one of the group of fifteen U-boats intercepted on 16 May when on passage from Vestfjord to Trondheim by the 9th (Canadian) Escort Group. The group arrived in Loch Eriboll at 2000 hours on 19 May. U-481 was boarded by a party from HMCS Monnow of the 9th (Canadian) Escort Group.

History after capture, and fate

U-481 was escorted from Loch Eriboll to Loch Alsh by the 9th Escort Group at 2020 hours on 20 May, arriving at 0730 hours the following day.

Towed out from Loch Ryan on 28 November 1945 by the tug Enforcer for destruction under Operation Deadlight. On 30 November the tow parted and U-481 was sunk by gunfire from Polish destroyer ORP Blyskawica at 5611N x 1000W later that day.

U-516

Type   IXC
Ordered   14 February 1940
Yard   Deutsche Werft AG, Hamburg
Job No.   312
Keel laid   12 May 1941
Launched   16 December 1941
Commissioned   21 February 1942

Circumstances of capture

Surfaced in the Bay of Biscay 275 miles west of St Nazaire on 10 May 1945 in response to the surrender radio transmissions. Intercepted by the 9th (Canadian) Escort Group off northern Scotland 14 May and separated from convoy JW 67. Per Pat Godwin, crew member of HMS Fitzroy, this U-boat surrendered to HMS Fitzroy of the 21st Escort Group. Escorted into Loch Eriboll at 1800 hours on 14 May.

History after capture, and fate

U-516 was escorted from Loch Eriboll at 0600 hours on 15 May and delivered to Loch Alsh by HMS Fitzroy, arriving at 1600 hours.

Towed out from Lisahally on 2 January 1946 as a target by HMS Quantock (L.58) for destruction under Operation Deadlight. En route to the final disposal point she foundered in heavy seas at 5606N x 0900W the same day.

U-532

Type   IXC/40
Ordered   15 August 1940
Yard   Deutsche Werft AG, Hamburg
Job No.   347
Keel laid   7 January 1942
Launched   26 August 1942
Commissioned   11 November 1942

Circumstances of capture

Surfaced on10 May 1945 between Iceland and the Western Approaches returning from the Far East carrying 8 tons wolfram, 5 tons molybdenum, 110 tons tin, 61 tons raw rubber and half a ton of quinine, strategic materials for the German war effort, having left Jakarta on 13 January. Per Pat Godwin, crew member of HMS *Fitzroy*, this U-boat surrendered to HMS *Rupert* of the 21st Escort Group. Escorted into Loch Eriboll at 1200 hours on 13 May.

History after capture, and fate

U-532 was escorted from Loch Eriboll at 2300 hours on 13 May and delivered to Loch Alsh by HMS *Rupert* at 1030 hours the following day. All but essential crew members were disembarked and *U-532* was then escorted to Gladstone Dock, Liverpool, nominally for the purpose of discharging the cargo (though this was not accomplished), arriving on 17 May. During this journey, escorted by HMS *Grindall* (K.477) and in foul weather, a German seaman was lost overboard after the boat was refused permission to submerge. From Liverpool *U-532* was taken to Vickers' Barrow Graving Dock, arriving on 25 May, opened for public inspection, and later delivered for storage in Loch Ryan to await her fate.

　　Towed out from Loch Ryan on 7 December 1945 by the tug *Masterful* for destruction under Operation Deadlight. *U-532* was sunk by torpedoes fired from HM Submarine *Tantivy* (P.319) on 9 December at 5608N x 1007W.

U-668

Type   VIIC
Ordered   15 August 1940
Yard   Howaldts Werke, Hamburg
Job No.   817
Keel laid   11 October 1941
Launched   5 October 1942
Commissioned   16 November 1942

Circumstances of capture

U-668 surrendered on 8 May 1945 in Norwegian waters and was one of the group of fifteen U-boats intercepted on 16 May on passage from Vestfjord to Trondheim by the 9th (Canadian) Escort Group. The group arrived in Loch Eriboll at 2000 hours on 19 May. *U-668* was boarded by a party from HMS *Byron* of the 21st Escort Group.

History after capture, and fate

U-668 was escorted from Loch Eriboll at 2000 hours to Loch Alsh on 21 May by HMS *Conn*, where she arrived at 0900 hours the following day.

　　Towed out from Lisahally on 31 December 1945 by HMS *Blencathra* (L.24) for destruction under Operation Deadlight. The tow parted on 1 January 1946 and *U-668* was sunk by gunfire from HMS *Onslaught* (G.04) at 5603N x 0924W that day.

U-716

Type   VIIC
Ordered   10 April 1941
Yard   Stulken Sohn, Hamburg
Job No.   782
Keel laid   16 April 1942
Launched   15 January 1943
Commissioned   15 April 1943

Circumstances of capture

U-716 surrendered on 8 May 1945 in Norwegian waters and was one of the group of fifteen U-boats intercepted at sea by the 9th (Canadian) Escort Group on 16 May when on passage from Vestfjord to Trondheim. The group arrived in Loch Eriboll at 2000 hours on 19 May. U-668 was boarded by a party from HMCS St Pierre of the 9th (Canadian) Escort Group.

History after capture, and fate

U-716 was escorted from Loch Eriboll at 2020 hours to Loch Alsh on 20 May 1945 by vessels of the 9th Escort Group, arriving at 0730 hours the following day.

Towed out from Loch Ryan on 9 December 1945 by HMS Rupert (K.561) for destruction under Operation Deadlight and expended as an aircraft bombing target by 248Sqn RAF on 11 December at 5550N x 1005W.

U-764

Type   VIIC
Ordered   15 August 1940
Yard   Kriegsmarinewerft, Wilhelmshaven
Job No.   147
Keel laid   1 February 1941
Launched   13 March 1943
Commissioned   6 May 1943

Circumstances of capture

Surfaced on13 May 1945 north of the Shetland Isles. Per Pat Godwin, crew member of HMS Fitzroy, this U-boat surrendered on 14 May to HMS Fitzroy. Escorted into Loch Eriboll at 1900 hours that day.

History after capture, and fate

U-764 was escorted from Loch Eriboll at 0600 hours on 15 May and delivered to Loch Alsh by HMS Deane, arriving at 1600 hours that day.

Towed out from Lisahally on 2 January 1946 by Polish destroyer ORP Krakowiak as torpedo target for HM Submarine Tantivy (P.319), but sunk by gunfire in heavy weather from Polish destroyer ORP Piorun at 5606N x 0900W the following day.

U-802

Type   IXC/40
Ordered   7 December 1940
Yard   Seebeckwerft, Bremerhaven
Job No   711
Keel laid   1 December 1941
Launched   31 October 1942
Commissioned   12 June 1943

Circumstances of capture

Surfaced and surrendered on 9 May 1945 south-west of Standtlandet island, (Norwegian coast north of Bergen), en route to the coast of USA. Per Pat Godwin, crew member of HMS *Fitzroy*, this U-boat was boarded by a party from HMS *Philante* acting as part of the 21st Escort Group. Escorted into Loch Eriboll at 1200 hours on 11 May.

History after capture, and fate

U-802 was escorted from Loch Eriboll at 0700 hours on 12 May and delivered to Loch Alsh by HMS *Deane* at 1500 hours that day.

Towed out from Lisahally on 30 December 1945 by HMS *Pytchley* (L.92) for destruction under Operation Deadlight. In foul weather the following day the tow parted and *U-802* was found to have disappeared, presumably foundered at approximately 5530N x 0825W.

U-825

Type   VIIC
Ordered   8 June 1942
Yard   F. Schichau, Danzig
Job No.   1588
Keel laid   19 July 1943
Launched   16 February 1944
Commissioned   4 May 1944

Circumstances of capture

Surfaced and surrendered on 10 May 1945 south-west of Ireland and photographed by a Wellington XIV of 172 Squadron from Limavady the following day 150 miles west of the coast of Donegal, heading north. Per Pat Godwin, crew member of HMS *Fitzroy*, this U-boat was boarded by a party from HMS *Byron* of the 21st Escort Group. Escorted into Loch Eriboll at 1100 hours on 13 May.

History after capture, and fate

U-825 was escorted from Loch Eriboll at 1245 hours on 13 May 1945 and delivered to Loch Alsh by HMS *Fitzroy*, arriving at 0730 hours the following day.

Towed out from Lisahally on 3 January 1946 by HMS *Mendip* (L.60) for destruction under Operation Deadlight, and sunk the same day by gunfire from Polish destroyer ORP *Blyskawica* when the tow parted at 5531N x 0730W.

U-826

Type   VIIC
Ordered   8 June 1942
Yard   F. Schichau, Danzig
Job No.   1589
Keel laid   6 August 1943
Launched   9 March 1944
Commissioned   11 May 1944

Circumstances of capture

Per Pat Godwin, crew member of HMS *Fitzroy*, *U-826* surrendered to HMS *Fitzroy* of the 21st Escort Group. Escorted into Loch Eriboll at 0600 hours on 11 May 1945.

History after capture, and fate

U-826 was escorted from Loch Eriboll at 1300 hours on 11 May and delivered to Loch Alsh by HMS *Fitzroy*, arriving at 2015 hours that day.

Towed out from Loch Ryan on 29 November 1945 by HMS *Pytchley* (L.92) for destruction under Operation Deadlight. Sunk by gunfire from HMS *Onslaught* (G.04) and Polish destroyer ORP *PioRun* on 1 December 1945 at 5610N x 1005W.

U-956

Type   VIIC
Ordered   10 April 1941
Yard   Blohm & Voss, Hamburg
Job No.   156
Keel laid   20 February 1942
Launched   14 November 1942
Commissioned   6 January 1943

Circumstances of capture

Surfaced 11 May 1945 off Northern Ireland. Per Pat Godwin, crew member of HMS *Fitzroy*, *U-956* surrendered to HMS *Byron* of the 21st Escort Group. Escorted into Loch Eriboll at 0900 hours on 12 May.

History after capture, and fate

U-956 was escorted from Loch Eriboll at 1245 hours on 13 May for Loch Alsh, arriving at 0730 hours the following day.

Towed out from Loch Ryan on 15 December 1945 as an aircraft bombing target by the tug *Prosperous* for destruction under Operation Deadlight. Sunk by naval gunfire on 17 December when the proposed air attack was cancelled, at 5550N x 1005W.

U-968

Type VIIC
Ordered 5 June 1941
Yard Blohm & Voss, Hamburg
Job No. 168
Keel laid 14 May 1942
Launched 4 February 1943
Commissioned 18 March 1943

Circumstances of capture

U-968 surrendered on 8 May in Norwegian waters and was one of the group of fifteen U-boats in-tercepted on 16 May when on passage from Vestfjord to Trondheim by the 9th (Canadian) Escort Group. *U-968* arrived in Loch Eriboll at 2130 hours on 19 May and was boarded by a party from HMCS *Matane* of the 9th (Canadian) Escort Group; the boarding party was photographed aboard the boat – see the photo illustrations in this book.

History after capture, and fate

U-968 was escorted from Loch Eriboll at 2020 hours to Loch Alsh by the 9th Escort group on 20 May 1945, arriving at 0730 hours the following day.
Towed out from Loch Ryan on 28 November 1945 by the tug *Prosperous* for destruction under Op-eration Deadlight. *U-968* foundered the next day and anchored its towing vessel to the seabed in 80 fathoms at 5524N x 0622W. The tow line had to be cut to save the towing vessel.

U-992

Type VIIC
Ordered 25 May 1941
Yard Blohm & Voss, Hamburg
Job No. 192
Keel laid 30 October 1942
Launched 24 June 1943
Commissioned 2 August 1943

Circumstances of capture

U-992 surrendered on 8 May in Norwegian waters and was one of the group of fifteen U-boats inter-cepted on 16 May when on passage from Vestfjord to Trondheim by the 9th (Canadian) Escort Group. The group arrived in Loch Eriboll at 2000 hours on 19 May. *U-992* was boarded by a party from a 9th (Canadian) Escort group frigate. The boat emblem included the three-letter call sign 'XUL'.

History after capture, and fate

U-992 was escorted from Loch Eriboll at 2000 hours to Loch Alsh by the 9th Escort Group on 21 May arriving at 0900 on 22 May. She was transferred to Lisahally on 10 June and returned to Loch Ryan on 1 September.
Towed out from Loch Ryan on 14 December 1945 by HMS *Fowey* (L.15) for destruction under Operation Deadlight and sunk by torpedoes fired from HM submarine *Tantivy* at position 5610N x 1005W the following day.

U-997

Type   VIIC/41
Ordered   14 October 1941
Yard   Blohm & Voss, Hamburg
Job No.   197
Keel laid   5 December 1942
Launched   18 August 1943
Commissioned   23 September 1943

Circumstances of capture

U-997 surrendered on 8 May in Norwegian waters and was one of the group of fifteen U-boats intercepted on 16 May when on passage from Vestfjord to Trondheim by the 9th (Canadian) Escort Group. The group arrived in Loch Eriboll at 2000 hours on 19 May. U-997 was boarded by a party from HMS Nene of the 9th (Canadian) Escort Group.

History after capture, and fate

U-997 was escorted from Loch Eriboll to Loch Alsh by the 9th Escort group at 2020 hours on 20 May, arriving at 0730 hours the following day.

Towed out from Loch Ryan on 9 December 1945 by the tug Bustler for destruction under Operation Deadlight, and sunk as an aircraft bombing target by 248Sqn RAF on 13 December at 5550N x 1005W.

U-1009

Type   VIIC/41
Ordered   23 March 1942
Yard   Blohm & Voss, Hamburg
Job No.   209
Keel laid   24 February 1943
Launched   5 January 1944
Commissioned   10 February 1944

Circumstances of capture

Surfaced and surrendered in the north Atlantic, between Shetland and the Faeroes, at 1200 hours on 9 May 1945. Later that day she was mistakenly attacked by an aircraft of Coastal Command, but continued her course towards Loch Eriboll.

Per Pat Godwin, crew member of HMS Fitzroy, this U-boat was the first to surrender to the 21st Escort Group and was boarded by a party from HMS Byron. Escorted into Loch Eriboll at 0700 hours on 10 May 1945. This was the first surrendered U-boat to enter any British base after the German armed forces' capitulation at the end of the Second World War.

History after capture, and fate

U-1009 was escorted from Loch Eriboll to Loch Alsh at 1300 hours on 10 May 1945 by HMS Byron, arriving at 0830 hours the following day.

Towed out from Loch Ryan on 15 December 1945 by HMS Mendip (L.60) for destruction under Operation Deadlight and sunk by naval gunfire from HMS Onslow (G.17) the following day at 5531N x 0724W.

U-1010

Type   VIIC/41
Ordered   23 March 1942
Yard   Blohm & Voss, Hamburg
Job No.   210
Keel laid   23 February 1943
Launched   5 January 1944
Commissioned   22 February 1944

Circumstances of capture

Surfaced in the north Atlantic on 5 May 1945 and set course for Loch Eriboll. Intercepted by the 9th (Canadian) Escort Group off northern Scotland 14 May and separated from convoy JW 67. Per Pat Godwin, crew member of HMS *Fitzroy*, this U-boat surrendered to HMS *Philante* with the 21st Escort Group. Escorted into Loch Eriboll at 1200 hours on 14 May.

History after capture, and fate

U-1010 was escorted from Loch Eriboll at 2150 hours on 14 May by HMS *Fitzroy* and delivered to Loch Alsh at 0800 hours the following day.

Towed out from Lisahally on 3 January 1946 by HMS *Loch Shin* (K.421) for destruction under Operation Deadlight. Had to be reboarded off Dungaree Point when the tow parted, and returned to Lisahally. Towed out for a second time, on 7 January 1946, by HMS *Quantock* (L.58) and when the tow parted for a second time *U-1010* was sunk by naval gunfire from Polish destroyer ORP *Garland* at 5537N x 0749W.

U-1058

Type   VIIC
Ordered   5 June 1941
Yard   Germaniawerft, Kiel
Job No.   692
Keel laid   2 August 1943
Launched   11 May 1944
Commissioned   10 June 1944

Circumstances of capture

Surfaced west of the Hebrides 9 May 1945 and made course for Loch Eriboll. Per Pat Godwin, crew member of HMS *Fitzroy*, this U-boat surrendered to HMS *Rupert* of the 21st Escort Group. Escorted into Loch Eriboll at 1600 hours on 10 May, the third U-boat to surrender.

History after capture, and fate

U-1058 was escorted from Loch Eriboll at 0700 hours on 11 May and delivered to Loch Alsh by HMS *Rupert* at 1600 hours that day.

Delivered to Lisahally for destruction under Operation Deadlight, but subsequently reprieved and handed over to the USSR as part of the Tripartite Agreement apportioning U-boats to the navies of the Allies. *U-1058* was delivered to the USSR in November from Lisahally by the Royal Navy, leaving on 24 November and arriving in Copenhagen on the 29th. A day later they left for Libau, Latvia, arriving on 5 December for handing over to the Soviet navy. The delivery of this and other former U-boats to the Soviet navy was named Operation Cabal.

U-1058 became H-23 of the Baltic Fleet with effect from 5 November 1945. On 9 June 1949 the vessel was renumbered S-82.

On 30 December 1955 the vessel was removed from the Soviet navy combat list, disarmed and converted to the floating auxiliary station PZS 82. On 25 March 1958 the vessel was excluded from the navy structure and scrapped.

U-1105

Type VIIC/41
Ordered 14 October 1941
Yard Noordsee Werke, Emden
Job No. 227
Keel laid 6 July 1943
Launched 20 April 1944
Commissioned 3 June 1944

Circumstances of capture

Surfaced off Cape Wrath and made passage for Loch Eriboll. Per Pat Godwin, crew member of HMS *Fitzroy*, this U-boat surrendered to HMS *Conn* of the 21st Escort Group off Loch Eriboll. Escorted in at 2000 hours on the 10 May 1945. This U-boat was known as 'The Black Panther' because of its external rubber coating.

History after capture, and fate (see also Postscript to this book)

U-1105 was escorted from Loch Eriboll at 0700 hours on 11 May by HMS *Rupert* and delivered to Loch Alsh, arriving at 1600 hours that day.

This boat was covered with an experimental thick rubber coating intended to help evade the Allied asdic and sonar detection equipment. Perhaps for that reason the vessel was never considered for destruction under Operation Deadlight, instead being retained by the Royal Navy for assessment and experimental purposes and renamed N-16.

Passed to the US Navy in 1946 for evaluation, and sunk in the Potomac River in September 1949. The wreck site became lost with the passage of time.

The boat was relocated in June 1985, to be designated Maryland's first historic shipwreck preserve.

U-1109

Type VIIC/41
Ordered 2 April 1942
Yard Noordsee Werke, Emden
Job No. 231
Keel laid 20 October 1943
Launched 19 June 1944
Commissioned 31 August 1944

Circumstances of capture

Per Pat Godwin, crew member of HMS *Fitzroy* this U-boat surrendered to HMS *Conn* of the 21st Escort Group. Escorted into Loch Eriboll at 1400 hours on 11 May.

History after capture, and fate

U-1109 was escorted from Loch Eriboll at 2300 hours on 12 May by HMS *Conn* and delivered to Loch Alsh, arriving at 0730 the following day.

Transferred to Lough Foyle and towed out from Lisahally on 5 January 1946 for destruction under Operation Deadlight by HMS *Zetland* (L.59). Sunk by a torpedo fired from HM Submarine *Templar* (P.316) on 6 January 1946 at 5549N x 0831W.

U-1165

Type   VIIC/41
Ordered   14 October 1941
Yard   Danziger Werft, Danzig
Job No.   137
Keel laid   31 December 1942
Launched   20 July 1943
Commissioned   17 November 1943

Circumstances of capture

U-1165 surrendered on 8 May 1945 in Norwegian waters and was one of the group of fifteen U-boats intercepted on 16 May when on passage from Vestfjord to Trondheim by the 9th (Canadian) Escort Group. The group arrived in Loch Eriboll at 2000 hours on 19 May. *U-1165* was boarded by a skeleton guard from HMS *Byron* of the 21st Escort Group.

History after capture, and fate

U-1165 was escorted from Loch Eriboll to Loch Alsh by HMS *Fitzroy* at 2000 hours on 21 May and arrived at 0900 hours the following day.

Towed out from Lisahally on 29 December 1945 by the Polish destroyer ORP *Krakowiak* for destruction under Operation Deadlight. The tow parted and *U-1165* returned to Moville under its own power. Towed out again by ORP *Krakowiak* on 30 December and sunk by gunfire from HMS *Offa* (G.29) the following day at 5544N x 0840W.

U-1231

Type   IXC/40
Ordered   14 October 1941
Yard   Deutsche Werft AG, Hamburg
Job No.   394
Keel laid   31 March 1943
Launched   18 November 1943
Commissioned   9 February 1944

Circumstances of capture

Surfaced bound for Gibraltar and set course for Loch Eriboll. Per Pat Godwin, crew member of HMS *Fitzroy*, this U-boat surrendered to HMS *Rupert* of the 21st Escort Group. Escorted into Loch Eriboll at 1600 hours on 13 May.

History after capture, and fate

U-1231 was escorted from Loch Eriboll at 2300 hours on 13 May and delivered to Loch Alsh by HMS *Rupert* at 1030 hours the following day.

Delivered to Lisahally for destruction under Operation Deadlight, but subsequently reprieved and handed over to the USSR as part of the Tripartite Agreement apportioning U-boats to the navies of the Allies. For details of the Royal Navy Operation Cabal, under which these vessels were delivered to the Soviet navy, see the data for *U-1058*.

U-1231 was renamed N-25 when absorbed into the Russian Navy in 1946. The boat is said to have been scrapped in 1960.

U-1305

Type   VIIC/41
Ordered   1 August 1942
Yard   Flensburger Schiffsbau
Job No.   498
Keel laid   30 July 1943
Launched   11 July 1944
Commissioned   13 September 1944

Circumstances of capture

Surfaced in the North-West Approaches and set course for Loch Eriboll. Per Pat Godwin, crew member of HMS *Fitzroy*, this U-boat surrendered to HMS *Deane* of the 21st Escort Group. Escorted into Loch Eriboll at 0800 hours on 10 May 1945, the second U-boat to surrender.

History after capture, and fate

U-1305 was escorted from Loch Eriboll at 1300 hours on 10 May by HMS *Deane* and delivered to Loch Alsh, arriving at 0830 hours the following day.

Delivered to Lisahally for destruction under Operation Deadlight, but subsequently reprieved and handed over to the USSR as part of the Tripartite Agreement apportioning U-boats to the navies of the Allies. For details of Operation Cabal, under which these vessels were delivered to the Soviet navy, see the data sheet for *U-1058*.

U-1305 became H-25 of the Baltic Fleet in February 1946, and on 9 July 1949 was renumbered S-84.

On 30 December 1955 the vessel was removed from the Soviet navy combat list, disarmed and converted to an experimental boat with the Northern Fleet. In October 1957 the boat sank during experiments with new weapon types near Novaya Zemlya, Arctic. On 1 March 1958 this boat was excluded from the navy structure whilst still on the bed of the Arctic Ocean.

U-2326

Type   XXIII
Ordered   20 September 1943
Yard   Deutsche Werft AG, Hamburg
Job No.   480
Keel laid   8 May 1944
Launched   17 July 1944
Commissioned   10 August 11944

Circumstances of capture

Surfaced in the North Sea between Aberdeen and Peterhead on 12 May 1945. A full description, by the commander, of the convoluted practicalities of this U-boat's surrender appears elsewhere in this book. Although there is compelling evidence that this boat had already surrendered and been boarded in Dundee on 14 May, and had been escorted to Loch Eriboll by a British frigate, per Pat Godwin, crew member of HMS *Fitzroy* this U-boat surrendered to HMS *Fitzroy*. Escorted into Loch Eriboll at 1130 hours on 18 May.

History after capture, and fate

U-2326 was escorted from Loch Eriboll at 1850 hours on 18 May and delivered to Loch Alsh by HMS *Fitzroy*, arriving at 0800 hours the following day. Escorted to Lisahally on 19 May by HMS *Kempthorne* (K.483).

Although delivered to Lisahally for storage alongside other Operation Deadlight candidates, this U-boat was retained by the British Navy and renamed HM Submarine N-35. After evaluation testing the U-boat was transferred to the French navy in 1946.

U-2326/N-35 sank on 6 December 1946 at Toulon in a deep-diving accident, with the loss of 17 lives. Although some sources claim that the wreck was raised to recover the bodies and scrapped, others point out that the French do not raise warships sunk with loss of life, preferring to regard them as military graves.

Section two

In addition to the thirty-three confirmed U-boats described above known and recorded as having been escorted into Loch Eriboll there are frequent references to additional boats having visited the northernmost deepwater sea loch in the weeks immediately after the end of the war. These 'possibles' usually number six in total and I have concentrated for the purposes of this exercise on those particular boats. Their stories are described below and are reasonably conclusive although, perhaps inevitably, there remain in some instances very slight possibilities of a closer Loch Eriboll association.

For the recorded facts emerging from detailed investigation into the following possible Loch Eriboll U-boat candidates I am grateful for the efforts of fellow U-boat researcher Martin Pegg, and for his permission to quote the results of his investigations here. Martin resides on the south coast of England and has relatively easy access to all of the principal naval archives, a definite advantage over my location in the far north of Scotland. He is an assiduous researcher and is to be commended for his tenacity and his willingness to share the results of his archival visits.

U-291

Type   VIIC
Ordered   5 June 1941
Yard   Bremer Vulkan, Bremen-Vegesack
Job No.   56
Keel laid   17 October 1942
Launched   30 June 1943
Commissioned   4 August 1943

Circumstances of capture

Surrendered on 5 May 1945 at Wilhelmshaven, Germany. According to the War Diary HMS *Dacres* (K.472) sailed on 23 June from Wilhelmshaven escorting a group of six surrendered U-boats including *U-291*, manned by skeleton crews, for British waters. By this date the U-boats would have been processed in Germany to remove all armaments, and thus there would have been no necessity to put into Loch Eriboll for these procedures to be carried out.

History after capture, and fate

The likelihood is that the U-boats were escorted via Scapa Flow, Shetland, direct to Loch Ryan for laying-up without a stopover in transit at Loch Eriboll, where reception facilities had been terminated some weeks earlier.

U-291 was towed out from Loch Ryan on 20 December 1945 by the Polish destroyer ORP *Krakowiak* for destruction under Operation Deadlight. En route to the final disposal point on 21 December the tow parted and *U-291* was sunk by gunfire from HMS *Onslaught* (G.04) at 5550N x 0908W.

U-720

Type   VIIC
Ordered   25 August 1941
Yard   Stulken Sohn, Hamburg
Job No.   786
Keel laid   17 August 1942
Launched   5 June 1943
Commissioned   17 September 1943

Circumstances of capture

U-720 surrendered on 7 May 1945 off Heligoland and put into Wilhelmshaven. The War Diary records that on 10 June U-720 continued to be impounded in Wilhelmshaven, along with a further eighteen surrendered U-boats. U-720 was sailed on 24 June 1945 for Loch Ryan, by-passing Loch Eriboll for the reasons stated above in relation to U-291.

History after capture, and fate

U-720 was towed out from Loch Ryan on 20 December 1945 by HMS Quantock (L.58) for destruction under Operation Deadlight and sunk by gunfire from HMS Onslaught (G.04), HMS Zetland (L.59), HMS Fowey (L.15) and Polish destroyer ORP PioRun the following day at 5604N x 0935W in over 500 fathoms.

U-868

Type   IXC/40
Ordered   25 August 1941
Yard   AG Weser, Bremen
Job No.   1076
Keel laid   11 March 1943
Launched   18 August 1943
Commissioned   23 December 1943

Circumstances of capture

Taken out of service 5 May 1945 in Bergen and surrendered on 8 May. On 16 May NOIC Bergen signalled to the British Admiralty that there were 35 German U-boats berthed in Bergen including U-868 and UD-5 (see later); of this total approximately 25 were fit for sea. On 17 May the total was increased to 26 with the discovery of U-228 half-submerged as a result of bomb damage. Four boats were reported as unserviceable due to enemy action or defects.

History after capture, and fate

On 29 May U-868 was escorted from Bergen by 30th Escort Group along with twelve other boats, all without torpedoes and manned by crews reduced to thirty medically examined men. Two days later it was reported that the group, including U-868 and UD-5 had arrived at Scapa. On 2 June the War Diary records that eight U-boats including U-868 escorted by HMS Loch Glendhu (K.619) and HMS Stockham (K.562) had left Scapa and were passing Cape Wrath. It was further reported two days later that the group of eight U-boats and their escorts had arrived in Loch Ryan.

U-868 was towed out from Loch Ryan on 28 November 1945 by the tug Saucy as an aircraft bombing target for destruction under Operation Deadlight, but sank in a steep dive when the tow-line parted on 30 November at 5548N x 0833W in 70 fathoms.

U-2529

Type   XXI
Ordered   6 November 1943
Yard   Blohm & Voss, Hamburg
Job No.   2529
Keel laid   29 September 1944
Launched   13 November 1944
Commissioned   22 February 1945

Circumstances of capture

Surrendered at Kristiansund, Norway, in May 1945 and, according to the ship's written service history, escorted from Norway on 1 June by HMS *Loch Eck* (K.422), to Loch Eriboll, arriving 3 June. (HMS *Loch Eck* formed part of Operation Doomsday, the force sent to undertake the reoccupation of Norway on 23 May 1945. Other frigates present were HMS *Bayntun* (K.310), HMS *Bahamas* (K.503) and HMS *Papua* (K.588). The force was commanded by destroyers HMS *Venomous* (D.75), on which German officers performed the official handover on 15 May, and HMS *Valorous* (D.82), despatched to Norway 14 May 1945 to undertake clearance operations prior to the entry of Allied personnel into Kristiansund south.)

History after capture, and fate

But the War Diary records the following slightly different sequence of events.

It was intended to sail *U-2529* alone from Kristiansund at 1400 on 3 June escorted by HMS *Loch Eck* expecting to arrive in Loch Eriboll on the morning of 5 June. But later on 3 June the C-in-C Home Fleet contacted the C-in-C Rosyth indicating that he required the ASW trawler HMS *Coldstreamer* (T.337) to rendezvous with HMS *Loch Eck* the following day. At the rendezvous HMS *Loch Eck* would proceed alone to Rosyth and HMS *Coldstreamer* would escort *U-2529* direct to Lisahally. The U-boat and escort were confirmed as arriving in Lisahally on 6 June.

U-2529 was selected for destruction under Operation Deadlight but was reprieved and taken over by the Royal Navy as HM Submarine N-27 and used for testing and evaluation trials.

In February 1946 *U-2529*/N-27 was transferred to the Soviet navy and redesignated B-28. Included in the Soviet navy lists until December 1955, when she began use as a static electric generator plant. Scrapped during 1958.

U-3017

Type   XXI
Ordered   6 November 1943
Yard   AG Weser, Bremen
Job No.   1176
Keel laid   2 September 1944
Launched   5 November 1944
Commissioned   5 January 1945

Circumstances of capture

U-3017 surrendered at Holmstrand, near Horten, Norway on 8 May 1945 after being subject to air attack three days earlier whilst on passage with a group of ten U-boats from Helsingor to Oslo. Left Horten on 18 May and arrived Oslo the same day.

History after capture, and fate

The whole group was inspected on 17 May, found to be disarmed and declared ready for sea. The intention was to move them to Oslo for further processing. A message dated 20 May confirmed the presence of the whole group in Oslo, disarmed and with reduced crew complements.

At 1900 on 3 June a group of six U-boats including *U-3017* was escorted from Oslo by frigates HMS *Montserrat* (K.586) and HMS *Papua* (K.588) using the swept channel route to the Pentland Firth and thence via the Minches and Lough Foyle to Lisahally, arriving on 7 June.

U-3017 replaced *U-2502* in July 1945 when the latter boat developed main motor trouble on passage to Cammell Laird's yard at Birkenhead for evaluation trials. *U-3017*, as one of the latest type XXI 'Elektro' boats, was not considered for inclusion in and destruction under Operation Deadlight in view of the vessel being almost new and evidently the latest design in U-boat development.

U-3017 was sailed from Lisahally on 8 August 1945 for Barrow shipyards, where she was dry-docked and closely inspected and evaluated. Redesignated HM Submarine N-41 and extensively sea-trialled. N-41 suffered a large accidental battery explosion during hydrogen content trials whilst in Vickers' Barrow yard on 29 August 1945. Returned to Lisahally 21 October 1945 and retained as a British submarine.

Scrapped November 1949 by John Cashmore Ltd, Newport, South Wales.

UD-5/O-27

Type   O 21 class, Royal Netherlands Navy
Ordered   8 July 1938
Yard   Rotterdamse Droogdok Maatschappij, Rotterdam
Job No.   K XXVII
Keel laid   3 August 1939
Launched   26 September 1941
Commissioned   30 January 1942

Circumstances of capture, and prior history

This vessel had an unusual early career, the many name changes making identification somewhat complicated – she had four identification numbers throughout her active life. She was ordered by the Royal Netherlands navy under the identification K (for *Kolonien*, a vessel intended for use in the Dutch colonies of the Far East) XXVII; at some time prior to 1940 the vessel was redesignated *O-27*. She fell into the hands of the invading German armed forces on the invasion of the Netherlands in May 1940.

The shipyard personnel scuttled the part-completed vessel. The intention to destroy the vessel completely was foiled by the swift occupation of the south bank of the Maas and the shipyards there. The German navy captured *O-27*, raised her and redesignated her *UD-5*. She was assigned to a training flotilla until commissioned. She undertook two Atlantic patrols between August 1942 and January 1943, attacking and sinking one Allied vessel. Thereafter she was returned to training and school-boat duties.

On 9 May 1945 *UD-5* surrendered at Bergen, Norway.

History after capture, and fate

Initial naval instructions were for *UD-5* to be escorted from Bergen on 24 May to Loch Eriboll. But the convoy of thirteen U-boats, escorted by 30th Escort Group, did not leave Bergen until 29 May and did not arrive in Scapa until 1330 hours on 31 May, by which time reception facilities in Loch Eriboll had been terminated. The group left Scapa at 0600 hours on 1 June and arrived in Lisahally the following day, a fact confirmed by a naval signal that day. So it is clear from this that the group sailed directly from Scapa to Northern Ireland, making no stops on the way.

Whilst in Lisahally *UD-5* was recognised as a former Dutch vessel and excluded from Operation Deadlight. A Dutch crew was despatched to Lisahally to repatriate her and she was sailed from there on 26 June arriving in Dundee on the 27th. It is just possible that *UD-5* did spend one unsupervised night in Loch Eriboll during this voyage, although I have as yet been unable to uncover any archive or documentary confirmation.

After an exchange of letters between Royal Netherlands naval personnel, *UD-5* was commissioned into the Royal Netherlands navy as *O-27* on 13 July 1945, fulfilling an intention which originated prior to the outbreak of the war. The vessel was in a very bad state of repair. After essential recommissioning works she was sailed back to the Netherlands where she was used as a torpedo trials and training boat in Den Helder.

On 8 February 1946 *O-27* was transferred to Rotterdam and in December was de-commissioned for maintenance and reconversion, in order to remove the Kriegsmarine equipment still installed.

On 10 May 1947 *O-27* was recommissioned into the Royal Netherlands navy, with pennant number S 807, as a torpedo trial boat.

O-27/S 807 was struck from the Navy lists on 14 November 1959, and on 23 December 1960 was sold for scrap to Jos De Smedt of Antwerp at a price of 131,000 guilders. She was broken up during 1961.

Life aboard a U-boat

No other vessel of war presented more difficult living conditions than those experienced in the close confines of a U-boat. Conditions were claustrophobic, irrespective of the size or class of the vessel. The ocean-going Atlantic boats were very much larger than coastal predators, but they carried many more mines and/or torpedoes and needed much larger crew numbers to operate them. All U-boats were noisy, fume-ridden, damp, confined and downright dangerous places in which to be incarcerated for any length of time.

War patrols could last between a few weeks and six months. Some patrols, to the Far-East for instance, extended to considerably longer than that. Crews generally were unable to bathe or shave and showers were wholly out of the question, as were changes of clothes. Crew members were expected to have only the clothes on their backs plus a change of underwear and socks. Laundering was impossible, and in any case there was no storage space for spare clothes for an entire crew. In equatorial latitudes opportunities for swimming might present themselves occasionally, but that certainly would not be an expected pleasure in the north Atlantic and the North Sea.

In addition to severe space constraints there was the constant problem of potable-water capacity. Fresh water was always strictly limited and rationed for drinking. These pressures would be so much greater when a water tank or tanks were filled with diesel fuel in order to extend the range of the boat for a particular patrol. Personal hygiene was restricted to a salt-water wash down employing a bucket and sponge. This was unpopular with crews, but nonetheless the only alternative. Special soap to counter the salt water was used, but it left a scummy residue on the skin. A cologne (Kolibri) was provided to control body odour, but it was at best only partially effective.

The crew of a U-boat was made up of specialists and seamen. Specialist crew members, such as radio men, torpedo men and machine mechanics were responsible for the correct maintenance and operation of the equipment aboard. These specialists (two or three qualified personnel for each specialisation) were typically on duty for three 4-hour shifts between 8.00 am and 8.00 pm; two 6-hour shifts operated through the night.

Ordinary seamen were responsible for all the remaining general duty tasks, such as loading and maintaining the torpedoes (these needed servicing every two or three days, including those deployed in the tubes ready for firing), bridge watches, operating deck guns and housekeeping duties, etc. Standing watch during stormy weather was never enjoyed by crewmen. Icy waves could and did sweep over the height of the conning tower, submerging the entire boat and drenching those on watch in the process. Men were clipped to rails inside the bridge to stop them being washed overboard and foul-weather clothing was provided (long jacket and trousers made of specially treated leather), but it could never be entirely successful in keeping watchkeepers dry. And, of course, the severely restricted space below made the drying of wet clothing impossible.

The personal space allocated to each crew member was always at a premium. One small locker had to accommodate the personal belongings of each man aboard. At the start of a patrol folding bunks needed to be employed in the forward torpedo room, until torpedoes had been expended, when more space became available. From then onwards torpedoes would be stored in their tubes ready for action and crews could use the space freed up, for sleeping. Very often there were fewer bunks available than crew numbers aboard; the only alternative was to resort to hot-bunking – as one person crawled out for duty, then the man he replaced crawled in.

Privacy was non-existent. Bunks were placed on each side of busy walkways and crew members were constantly passing fore and aft along the narrow boat. Only the commander was afforded any degree of privacy, and then only by means of a simple curtain drawn across the access to his restricted private quarters. The captain's private space was always adjacent to the control room, so that he might immediately respond to any emergency.

Food aboard a U-boat could be both the best and the worst the military had to offer. At the start of a patrol fresh meat and vegetables, fruit, bread and dairy products would be available, and relished by everyone aboard. Provisions would be crammed into every last nook and cranny available, and even the second toilet space would be utilised to capacity for food storage. But the small refrigerators on board, combined with the constantly damp atmosphere, meant that food spoiled quickly. Fresh bread (*Kommissbrot*) would soon sprout a white fungus, a condition nicknamed 'rabbits' by the crews. As fresh food became used up or contaminated it was superseded by canned provisions. A soya-based bread substitute, *Bratlingspulver*, provided an alternative staple. Crews referred to it as 'diesel food', an acknowledgement of the constant diesel exhaust fumes in which they existed and of which everything tasted.

Toilet arrangements took on their own peculiar significance. Until the food stocks in the second toilet compartment had been used up, only one usable toilet was available for use by perhaps fifty men. Unfortunate emergency situations did occur. The flush system consisted of a hand-operated pump which ejected the waste direct into the ocean. This precluded use during preparations for an attack, as it was considered that the unavoidable metallic noises generated during use of the flushing mechanism might well reveal the presence of a U-boat, and any floating debris certainly would.

Long war cruises inevitably took a psychological toll. The constant emptiness of the ocean with its absence of trees and geographical features, and no opportunity to stretch one's legs other than on the external deck of the boat, left the crew in dire need of sensory stimulation. There would be excitement enough when stalking a target or being hunted themselves, but in the long periods of silence and inactivity when submerged crews would have only the U-boat's record player, or cards, to break the monotony. Some commanders organised compulsory singing or even lying contests to stimulate their crews and to provide diversion.

In his very revealing book *The Fuhrer Led, But We Overtook Him*, describing his service aboard the one captured U-boat assimilated into the British navy during the war years (Type VIIC *U-570*, captured on her maiden patrol on 27 August 1941 in the north Atlantic, south of Iceland, sailed back to Britain and renamed HMS *Graph*, the name given to the retrieval operation), Phil Durham describes the discomforts for which U-boat designs were notable.

> Their crews were forced to live in conditions which, if imposed on farm animals, would likely have involved prosecution for cruelty. In cramped quarters with inefficient sanitary arrangements, meagre fresh water supplies and even officers', petty officers', and engine room artificers' messes bisected by an open corridor, there was no privacy and seamen and stokers ate and slept in any corner of the deck they could find. On the surface, with its limited buoyancy, the boat bucketed about so violently in rough weather that it was not possible to stand or move about without holding on.

By the end of a war patrol bearded crews would emerge with soiled, stained and foul-smelling uniforms and a generally repellent aura. But they were always welcomed back to their bases with music and celebration. Success pennants were flown by the returning U-boat to signify the number of 'kills' during that patrol. Admiral Doenitz had great respect for his returning U-boat crews; he knew what they had been through and he knew what life aboard an operational U-boat was like.

Life Aboard a U-boat

Personal hygiene for crew engaged in any U-boat patrol always presented great problems. There was little water storage capacity, and all of that was reserved for drinking water. Showers were therefore out of the question; the best that could be offered was a wash-down with sea-water and a sponge using a special soap, which left a scummy residue on the skin. 'Kolibri' cologne was used to overcome body odour, but it was only ever marginally effective (David Oearn/www.uboataces.com)

Service aboard a U-boat provided both the best and the worst food available. At the start of the patrol plentiful supplies of fresh food were loaded, but these were either soon exhausted or spoiled in the damp atmosphere aboard. These two photographs show fresh bread and other consumables being loaded for storage into any tiny space available. For the majority of the patrol U-boat crews subsisted on tinned or re-hydrated provisions. (David Oearn/www.uboataces.com)

Accommodation on board was extremely cramped. There was no storage provision and all crew were expected to take only the clothes they were wearing plus a change of underwear and socks. There was no clothes-drying or hanging space. Before torpedoes were expended crewmembers were obliged to use folding cots in the torpedo room. Even then there were often fewer beds than ratings aboard, and hot-bunking was unavoidable (David Oearn/www.uboataces.com)

Left: Diversions to occupy the crew during the long submerged voyages or oppressive silent periods were vital to maintain crew morale. Board games provided some mental stimulus, as did gramophone records and books; some commanders organised lying contests to break the monotony until the next period of frantic action (David Oearn/www.uboataces.com)

Middle and right: These two photographs show the very limited space aboard the Type IXC/40 U-boat, illustrating the privations endured by the crew. The area next to the torpedo tubes and the restricted crew space are pictured (Author's collection)

A 'trot' (the navy's term) of four U-boats moored at Loch Ryan towards the end of 1945, awaiting their fate (Imperial War Museum)

Five U-boats pictured in Loch Ryan on 30 November 1945 immediately prior to their destruction under Operation Deadlight. Eighty-six U-boats were stored in Loch Ryan. All the boats selected for destruction had been towed to the scuttling point by the end of December (Associated Press courtesy Richard Holme)

Lisahally

Captain class frigate HMS Torrington escorts U-293 (leading) and U-1009 (following) upstream in the river Foyle, approaching Lisahally, Lough Foyle, Northern Ireland on 14 May 1945 (Imperial War Museum)

A fine study dated 14 May 1945 showing U-1009 – with crew members smartly at attention on deck and bridge beneath the White Ensign – entering Lisahally (Imperial War Museum)

Above: U-1058 pictured at speed approaching Lisahally for the surrender ceremony (Author's collection)

Left: U-826 securing at Lisahally, 14 May 1945, prior to the formal 'surrender' ceremony enacted – perhaps for the benefit of the assembled local press and population – in the presence of Sir Max Horton, Commander in Chief Western Approaches (Imperial War Museum)

Operation Deadlight

A British naval tug tows one of the Type XXIII 'Elektro' U-boats away from Lough Foyle for destruction in the north Atlantic under Operation Deadlight. All of the U-boats were sunk with engines and gear intact (Amalgamated Press/Author's collection)

Above: A group of large ocean-going U-boats awaits its fate in Loch Ryan. U-776 (Type VIIC), nearest the camera, undertook a tour of the British east coast ports in May and June 1945. It was manned by a British crew to enable members of the public to tour the boat. Huge numbers of visitors passed through the boat and thousands of pounds were raised for naval charities. She was towed from Loch Ryan on 3 December 1945 by the tug Enforcer *and foundered that day (Amalgamated Press/Author's collection)*

Right: U-2335 *received a direct hit from HMS* Onslaught *on 28 November 1945 and sank in deep water (Amalgamated Press/Author's collection)*

Left: On board U-2321 *electric impulse fuses are adjusted so that they can be fired by wire from the escorting destroyer, though in the event this U-boat was sunk by gunfire on 27 November 1945 jointly by the British destroyer HMS* Onslow *and the Polish destroyer ORP* Blyskawica *(Amalgamated Press/Author's collection)*

Below: The scene in Loch Ryan at the commencement of Operation Deadlight in late November 1945. A British destroyer, HMS Cubitt, *tows a U-boat for sinking in the north Atlantic. Many boats foundered or had to be destroyed short of the preferred target area because of terrible weather (Amalgamated Press/Author's collection)*

U-1165 *seen picking up the tow from Lisahally from the Polish destroyer ORP* Krakowiak *on 30 December 1945. HMS* Offa *sank the U-boat by gunfire the following day (Author's collection)*

OPERATION DEADLIGHT

I do not propose that this chapter will be either a definitive or an exhaustive study of the entire British operation over the winter of 1945–46 designed to solve the question of the captured German submarine fleet and of what to do with it. There are excellent studies published that dissect the whole scheme and which provide precise details of how and why the arrangements were formulated in their eventual form. All I aim to achieve here is to provide a basic overview, coloured with the use of contemporary documents and reports from those present. The situation was unique. The problems it presented had never been encountered previously and would certainly never occur again.

In November 1945, six months after the end of hostilities, the British naval authorities held the vast majority of the captured U-boats. Approximately 154 individual vessels survived the war to be surrendered or otherwise transferred to the safe-keeping of the Allies. Those surviving in the European theatre of operations were sailed to British ports for storage until a decision could be agreed on as to their fate.

Approximately thirty U-boats were apportioned between the Allies under a tripartite agreement of 3 November 1945. The British, United States and Russian navies were each allocated a number of vessels from the various types of U-boats – long-range open-sea attack vessels or coastal predators operating much nearer to their flotilla bases. Details of this initial apportionment and of the total numbers of vessels involved appear elsewhere in this work. It should be noted that at this stage in the immediate post-war period, U-boats were not allocated to the French; the British unilaterally decided that vessels should be turned over to the French from the British allocation.

It is difficult to be dogmatic about the specific numbers of captured vessels involved in the various disposal and dispersal agreements drawn up during 1945. The French government continually argued for a seat at the negotiating table, the first rumblings of the Cold War and a simmering distrust of Soviet intentions were beginning to manifest themselves, and even disputes between apparently closely allied victorious national governments all contributed to a continually evolving atmosphere where self-interest and prestige played an increasing part in an already fluid situation.

When quoting the total numbers of U-boats destroyed during the winter of 1945–46, an exercise subject to the closest scrutiny and for which evidently precise records were maintained, the historical record has become fogged not only by interpretation and supposition but also by a certain degree of difference between the intended destruction candidates and the actual. This should not be so, since contemporary official documents record in minute detail the sequence of events and the identities of those impounded U-boats destroyed. The following narrative quotes figures and other relevant data used in the official memoranda of the time.

In addition to the 150 or so U-boats surrendered to the Allies at the end of hostilities, there were a further 232 vessels (as near as can be ascertained) in German ports or under German influence which were scuttled before they could fall into enemy hands. On 30 April 1945 Admiral Doenitz, Commander-in-Chief of the German naval forces, issued a decree that in order to preserve the honour of the Kriegsmarine all vessels of the fleet should be scuttled immediately on receipt of the code word *Regenbogen* (Rainbow). The only exceptions to this order for self-destruction were vessels which could be employed in fishing, for transport and in mine clearance.

The increasingly hopeless military struggle was kept going for a few days after the issue of the scuttling authority so that men, refugees, supplies and equipment could be repatriated, and to ensure that his Kriegsmarine commanders would have available more time and opportunity to prepare their vessels for scuttling. But at 1514 hours on 4 May Doenitz was forced to withdraw the order by Allied commanders as a condition of the agreed surrender of all German armed forces. U-boat commanders in the western Baltic, however, believed this countermanding order to be against the will of Doenitz, and scuttled their vessels before surrendering themselves and their crews.

Of these 232 U-boats scuttled by their commanders, just 16 were aged or damaged vessels which had been paid off and were therefore not in commission and a further 5 were in the final stages of commissioning and therefore non-operational. Operation *Regenbogen* claimed many more operational U-boats than were ever delivered to the Allied forces as part of the capitulation arrangements.

On the morning of the 4 May 1945 Admiral Doenitz issued the following signal to all U-boat commanders:

> ALL U-BOATS. ATTENTION ALL U-BOATS.
> CEASE FIRE AT ONCE. STOP ALL HOSTILE ACTION AGAINST ALLIED SHIPPING.
> DOENITZ.

Approximately sixty-two U-boats were at sea when this 'end hostilities' order was issued. Of these vessels, fifty-four surrendered to Allied or neutral ports. It could be argued that had the countermand to the *Regenbogen* order been issued before or as part of the 'cease fire' order, then there might well have been significantly fewer scuttlings in the Baltic by U-boat commanders. But in view of what was to follow, the end result would doubtless have been the same.

In early November those U-boats to be retained by the Allied forces for evaluation and testing had been identified and the question of what to do with the remainder and how to accomplish that end needed to be determined urgently. It seems that the British Government was adamant from quite an early stage that the captured vessels would be permanently destroyed. Whether this was intended as retribution for the dreadful damage that the U-boat war had inflicted upon Allied shipping, or being mindful of the scuttling of the German Grand Fleet in Scapa Flow after the First World War and of the similar action in the western Baltic at the immediate end of the Second World War, remains a question to be decided by historians with greater knowledge than myself.

But the fact remains that in November 1945 the decision to put the captured U-boats then under the control of the Royal Navy beyond all reach had been taken. That decision was underpinned by a strong determination to carry out the intention with all possible haste. November was perhaps not the most auspicious time to initiate what was certainly a hazardous plan, but Operation Deadlight had been formulated to settle the question once and for all. The plan called for each of the captured U-boats to be towed into the Atlantic Ocean and consigned to the deep using explosive charges, gunfire, aircraft bombing, torpedo attack, or by means of the then top-secret 'Squid' ship-to-ship missile. The Tripartite Naval Agreement for the allocation of captured U-boats to the Allied navies was formulated on 3 November. Two days later methods of disposal for the remainder were discussed.

On 14 November the Office of the Commander-in-Chief, Rosyth, Fife issued memorandum number 3552/00968XR/A/2(d), headed 'Operation Deadlight'. The document ran to ten typed pages, each one of which was headed 'Confidential'; copies were circulated widely to eminently senior Royal Navy and Royal Air Force personnel. The preamble gave a clear indication of the sensitivity the naval authorities knew surrounded the intentions, since it stressed the unequivocal instruction 'These orders are to be complied with on receipt of the signal "Carry out Operation Deadlight", and are to be destroyed on completion of the operation'.

Paragraph 1 stated that there were 86 U-boats at Loch Ryan and 24 U-boats at Lisahally, the port for Londonderry, Northern Ireland; that no U-boat would have any crew on board and therefore all would require towing to the disposal point. HMS *Nairana* would be stationed in the vicinity of position 55.50N x 10.05W to co-ordinate and control air practices and to act as the weather-reporting ship.

Reference positions:

Datum position XX	56.00N	10.05W
U-boat air target position ZZ	55.50N	10.05W
Main scuttling position YY	56.10N	10.05W

Distance table:

Loch Ryan to position XX	180 miles
Moville (Lough Foyle) to position XX	130 miles

Intention:

To tow all U-boats from Loch Ryan and Lisahally to the vicinity of position YY or XX and scuttle them in these positions, completing the operation in the shortest possible time and taking every advantage of favourable weather.

During this operation, should weather conditions be favourable for air operations, to provide air practices for Fleet Air Arm and Coastal Command, RAF personnel, with U-boat targets, but accepting no delay in the scuttling of the U-boats.

Should weather conditions be favourable, to provide U-boat targets for non-contact pistol trials using submarines of the Third Submarine Fleet.

The Method of Execution stipulated that C-in-C Rosyth would be in general command, that Captain (Submarines) Loch Ryan and Naval Officer-in-Charge, Londonderry would assume immediate command of operations from Loch Ryan and Lisahally respectively, and were to issue orders as required. Loch Ryan would be cleared of U-boats first. Escort vessels and tugs would then sail to Moville to complete the Lisahally clearance.

U-boats would be towed by double bridles at no more than seven knots for Type XXIII boats and not exceeding eight knots for all other U-boat types. Conning-tower hatches were to be closed in Type XXIIIs and left open in all others. Towing vessels were to endeavour to recover their own tow lines; U-boat tows were to be sunk with the boat. 'In the event of a towing vessel parting her tow, and recovery being impracticable, the U-boat was to be sunk where she was, provided she would not be a danger to navigation. The position was to be accurately fixed.'

The method of scuttling was to be by safety fuse if weather conditions were suitable for boarding, with charges placed so as to collapse the bow and stern torpedo tubes and also to blow certain other hatches. Should weather conditions be unsuitable for boarding then scuttling charges were to be fired electrically. In the event of both suggested methods failing, the towing vessel was to sink the U-boat.

Escort vessels were authorised to sink U-boats by gunfire, Shark projectiles or Squid missiles. Depth charges were not to be used. Squid missiles were to be set to twenty feet manually.

From each group of U-boats sailing, three were to be detailed as targets for air practices. These target U-boats were to be identified by a broad white band painted athwartships on the forecastle. Air target U-boats were to be taken to position ZZ, the remainder to position YY. If aircraft failed to sink a designated practice target U-boat it may be sunk by accompanying vessels by gunfire and/or Squid. Squid was *not* to be used when members of the press or foreign observers were present, or any other vessel was within watching distance of the Squid deployment.

There were several appendices to the memorandum, but for the purposes of this section by far the most interesting is Appendix A, which identified which U-boats were to be destroyed from each of the two mooring locations.

Appendix 'A'

Lisahally

Type VIIC	**244**	**278**	**294**	**363**	**668**	**764**	**825**	901	
	930	**1010**	1022	**1109**	**1165**				= 13
IXC	**516**	541	**802**						= 3
IXD2	861	874	875	883					= 4
XXIII	2336	2341							= 2
XXI	2506	2511							= 2
								TOTAL	= 24

Loch Ryan

Type VIIC	245	249	**255**	281	291	**293**	**295**	298	
	299	**312**	**313**	**318**	328	368	369	**427**	
	481	483	485	637	680	**716**	720	739	
	760	773	775	776	778	779	**826**	907	
	928	**956**	**968**	978	991	**992**	994	**997**	
	1002	1004	1005	**1009**	1019	1052	1102	1103	
	1104	1110	1163	1194	1198	1203	1271	1272	
	1301	1307							= 58
Type VIID	218								= 1
Type VIIF	1061								= 1
Type IXC	155	170	**532**	539	856	868	1230	1233	= 8
Type XXIII	2321	2322	2324	2325	2328	2329	2334	2335	
	2337	2345	2350	2354	2361	2363			= 14
Type II	143	145	149	150					= 4
								TOTAL	= 86

(**Bold** type indicates U-boats *confirmed* at Loch Eriboll)

RAF Groups 18 and 19 were to deploy Sunderland, Warwick, Liberator and Mosquito or Beaufighter aircraft from bases at Lossiemouth, Kinloch, East Fortune and Alness for air practice exercises. Fleet Air Arm aircraft from either Machrihanish or HMS *Nairana* were similarly involved.

Operation Deadlight commenced on 25 November 1945 and ended on 12 February 1946. In that period 116 former German submarines were disposed of in the planned programme of destruction. The reasons for the differing total numbers of boats destroyed might be a little better understood when one realises that in the event, from Lishally, *thirty* U-boats were destroyed and not the twenty-four detailed in the document quoted above. The additional candidates were: *U-1023* (Type VIIC) sunk on 8 January 1946, *U-2502* (Type XXI) sunk on 3 January, *U-2356* (Type XXIII) sunk on 6 January, and *U-2351* (Type XXIII) sunk on 3 January. An additional U-boat (*U-3514*) was also identified for destruction but was retained pending the safe arrival of *U-3515* in Russia. Data on these amended totals were extracted from the report prepared on 26 January 1946 by Captain N.A. Richard RN, Naval Officer-in-Charge of the Lisahally operation.

Other U-boats were present, and those scheduled for delivery to the Russian navy under Operation Cabal, plus further vessels which were to become United States prizes, were at some time stored in Lough Foyle. It is clear that further U-boat destructions were undertaken from Lisahally after Captain Richard compiled his report of 26 January – see the report later in this section which describes the events of 9–12 February 1946.

Much myth and confusion concerning the facts of the disposal have been generated over the past sixty or more years. Perhaps, therefore, it might be advisable to quote from contemporary documents describing or referring to the actual sequence of events.

Volume 9, number 223 of *The War Illustrated*, dated 4 January 1946, contains a first-hand if somewhat jingoistic account (not entirely unexpected, in view of the privations of the war years) of the destruction of Operation Deadlight U-boats as seen from the Loch Ryan perspective. The report is quoted here verbatim:

Operation Deadlight: sinking the U-boat fleet

Germany's submarines are putting to sea for the last time: we are scuttling them in the Western Approaches, where so many merchant ships were attacked and sent to the bottom by them during the war. Witnessing these operations in the Atlantic, Gordon Holman has written this account specially for *The War Illustrated*.

The final chapter of the story of the longest battle of the war is entitled 'Operation Deadlight'. It is being written now, eight months after the end of the war with Germany, in the grey bleakness of the north Atlantic where most of the story was unfolded over five and a half long years. 'Operation Deadlight', which began on November 25th 1945, puts into effect the plan for the destruction of all surplus U-boats. It is a plan which has received the approval of the major Allied powers.

A large proportion of the German underwater fleet which carried on unrestricted warfare against our shipping from the time of the sinking of the *Athenia* on the night of September 3rd 1939, until the end of the hostilities had been assembled in two

British ports. Some of the U-boats had been brought in straight from the sea after surrendering to British surface forces. Others had made the passage from German ports, following closely the course of the German fleet that had straggled into Scapa Flow twenty-six years earlier. The fate of the U-boats was to be the same as that of the surface ships after the previous war – but now the scuttling was to be done for them.

Loch Ryan, in south-west Scotland, which, with Stranraer at its head, was the main point of assembly for the U-boats. Eighty-six of them were lying there when I arrived in the Polish destroyer *Blyskawica*. They were in little groups of five and six, which made the fleet appear deceptively small until one got among the craft. Twenty-four other U-boats were at Lisahally, on the northern Irish coast. These two collections made up the total of 110 surplus U-boats.

To move among the larger force of submarines in Loch Ryan was a strange experience. Here was three-quarters of what remained of a fleet that had menaced our very existence as an island people. These craft, and others like them already sunk, had imposed a never-to-be-forgotten toll on the Allied navies and merchant navies. But for the unfailing devotion to duty that we have come to expect from our seamen, they might have snatched victory for Hitler even when he had little to hope for in other directions.

In Loch Ryan, in the autumn of the same year that many of them had been on active operations against us, they looked fairly harmless, although one felt there was a lot to be said for putting them where they would remain harmless for all time. To almost anybody who has sailed the seas in times of war, a submarine has sinister suggestions. There was little need to extend the imagination in this direction when passing among clusters of them, many with their 'U' markings still on their conning towers.

An American-built Captain class frigate acted as guard ship, but most of the U-boats were unmanned. A crew of about 40 men had been permitted to remain on the centre boat of each cluster. They not only looked after their own craft but supplied working parties to carry out necessary maintenance on the vessels alongside them. At the appointed time, the U-boats would move slowly down the loch under their own power until they were finally abandoned by their crews and taken in tow for the 'burial ground' in the Atlantic.

Each cluster of U-boats had one White Ensign flying over it and two signal pennants which were identification numerals. There was no uniformity in the way the submarines had been brought together. *U-313*, a big transport craft with a flat deck the size of a Thames pleasure boat almost hid *U-2335* and *U-2329*, two Mark 23 submarines with which the Germans made their final desperate inshore attacks on our shipping.

A rusty square radar installation stood out above the conning tower of *U-170*, another big boat – probably of 1,500 tons. *U-360* had an odd, mottled appearance where large splashes of red lead had been slapped across her hull. One trot (the Navy's name for these clusters of craft) was impressive because five large U-boats of the same pattern were all lying side by side.

Many of the larger boats had double gun platforms but the guns were missing. One wonders what grim actions had been fought against the RAF or Fleet Air Arm from these gun positions. The little U-boats, with their hulls hardly showing above the still waters of the Loch, had no gun platforms at all. Their defence was their smallness and the readiness with which they could be taken down and, with the aid of their Snorkel air tubes, kept down.

Symbol of end of Nazi sea power

Along the single wire rigging running fore and aft from the conning towers, the last of the German crews had hung their washing. Few of the men who would remain to see their boats towed away to final destruction were on deck. One small party was busy, however, with welding apparatus. They were preparing for the last tow. As we drew away from the fleet of U-boats and their grey hulls became merged in the background of the Scottish hills, the blue welding flame stood out vividly. Suddenly it flickered and was gone – a strange symbol of the end of German sea power.

On November 25th the first towing operation began. In command of the group of ships taking part was Captain StJ. A. Micklethwaite, holder of three DSOs, who was a prisoner in the hands of the Germans for three years. He was captured after his ship, HMS *Sikh*, had been sunk in the Mediterranean. Now, in command of the famous destroyer HMS *Onslow*, he led the U-boat funeral procession.

From the bridge on which Captain R. St V. Sherbrooke fought on to win the VC after he had been badly wounded, Captain Micklethwaite gave his orders for the disposal of the U-boats. *Onslow* led the destroyers which, on the last day of 1942, in the Arctic twilight, four times placed themselves between the convoy they were guarding and a greatly superior force of enemy ships. For Operation Deadlight, *Onslow* still bore her proud motto '*Festina Lente*' – 'Hasten Slowly', or, as the sailors invariably translate it, 'On Slow'. Other ships in this first towing were the Polish destroyer *Blyskawica* (British-built before the war), the Hunt Class destroyer HMS *Southdown*, the British-built frigate HMS *Cubitt* and four tugs.

The U-boats going out to be scuttled, six of the small Mark 23 type craft, were brought down to the towing ships by skeleton crews provided by the Royal Navy, with four Germans in addition. As each boat was taken in tow, it was allowed to run out until the strain was on the tow, and then the crew was taken off. There was no ceremony of farewell for the Germans. They were taken ashore at once and probably did not see their craft slowly head out to sea.

Heavy strain on towing gear

The chosen scuttling-ground was where the Atlantic bed shelves away sharply about a hundred miles north-west of Lough Swilly and 80 miles north-west of the Bloody Foreland in Donegal. Here there is a depth of about a thousand fathoms and it was felt that there was no chance of any part of the submarines, or such fuel and oil as remained on board, coming to the surface or otherwise interfering with fishing.

Progress to this area was necessarily slow. The unmanned submarines placed a heavy strain on the towing gear, especially in the long swell encountered in the open Atlantic. Proceeding at four knots, the force arrived early on the morning of the second day after leaving Loch Ryan. An hour or so before this, HMS *Cubitt* reported to the *Onslow* that the U-boat she was towing had disappeared; she had foundered.

Number one plan for the destruction of the U-boats called for the firing of three high explosive charges already fitted into the U-boats. In order to carry the electric impulse to these charges it was necessary to pick up a line trailing from each U-boat. The destroying ships were HMS *Onslow* and the *Blyskawica*.

A fairly heavy sea was running, but by fine seamanship the *Onslow* was able to get close to *U-2361* and pick up the line. In a matter of minutes a connexion had been made, and the *Onslow* went astern until she was about 1,000 feet from the doomed U-boat. Then a plunger was pressed home and, in a triple explosion, both ends of the submarine were blown out and debris flung high in the air from the conning tower. When the smoke cleared the U-boat had vanished.

Meantime, *Blyskawica*, putting into effect the second method of destruction, had opened fire on the first of her victims, *U-2321*. A few rounds accounted for this craft; and the Polish gunners had even more spectacular success with their second U-boat, sinking it with four quick rounds.

Onslow then sank her second U-boat by gunfire, and this was quickly followed by a third disposed of in the same way by the Poles. Shells screamed into the submarines at close range, tearing conning towers wide open and penetrating the hulls. By midday the first batch of U-boats had settled down in the burial ground and the *Onslow* was leading the 'destroyers' back for more at a steady twenty knots. Before dark signals were exchanged with the *Onslow*'s sister ship HMS *Onslaught*, heading a second group of ships with their sleek tows to the sinking grounds.

This account of the sinking of the first batch of U-boats does not convey the problems encountered later in the exercise. Bad weather was responsible for the loss of many U-boats in less than ideal circumstances. The fifth batch of U-boats left Loch Ryan on 3 December 1945, the commanding officer later being obliged to report that none of his charges reached the preferred sinking point, for each one foundered en route:

When I slipped at 1400, Loch Ryan was suffering what the Admiralty forecast termed as a polar air stream. Gusts from the NNW of force 3 brought dense hailstones which added to the difficulties of the towing ships in getting under way. The situation developed even more rapidly than on the two former occasions. At 1415 *Southdown* reported that she has been savaged by her U-boat [...] 'having a broken frame, and one plate split'. I ascertained that she was seaworthy and she proceeded to sea though she had considerable trouble in turning to leave harbour and came out badly astern of the remainder.

At 1416 *Mendip* reported that she had parted her tow in a position five cables north of Meilleur Point. She had not the gear to resume towing and was ordered to anchor by Captain S/M. I hailed Lt Commander Weston RN who was busy chasing submarines in a motor boat and he proceeded to the scene of the disaster accompanied by the harbour tug *Empire Ivy*. When last seen he was steaming the U-boat back to Cairnryan and appeared to be single-handedly combining the functions of captain and crew (all departments).

I now received an appeal for assistance from *Obedient*. He was lying stern to seaward, his U-boat engines had broken down and he was quite unable to turn.

At 1855 *Enforcer* reported that his tow might have parted. The tug was lying astern to the wind anchored by his tow. *Enforcer* was ordered to burn through his tow, buoy the position and return to Loch Ryan.

The night brought navigational difficulties, but all U-boats continued to float. The weather deteriorated rapidly before an intense depression off the west coast of Ireland, and by dawn the wind had reached force 8. The greatest difficulty was experienced in steering. The circus became somewhat untidy straggling over a large expanse of the North Channel.

I had the gravest misgivings as to the hopes of all ships navigating the passage in safety; however by 1140/4 the rear ship was through. While going rounds it was observed that further incidents were imminent. *Southdown*'s U-boat was down by the stern (the navigation lights had gone out at 0750) as was *Saucy*'s. The one towed by *Cubitt* was badly down by the bows and speculation was rife as to which would go first. *U-218* (*Southdown*) went to the bottom stern first at 1205 and *U-778* (*Cubitt*) not to be outdone lunged under bow first at 1228. At 1845 *Saucy* reported that her tow had sunk, being observed to founder by three officers.

In the meantime *Blyskawica* and *Obedient* were searching for *Obedient*'s U-boat which had broken adrift at 1750. *Fowey* was ordered to proceed to position ZZ independently and to act under the orders of *Nairana* on arrival. *Fowey*'s U-boat had appeared to be in good health at 2000 but at 2027 she reported that it was behaving very sluggishly and it foundered at 0002. At 0650 she (*Prosperous*) reported undue strain on her tow and it was observed to sink at 0703.

The operation having thus been unsuccessfully completed I ordered her to return to Loch Ryan. (Richard Holme, *Cairnryan: Military Port 1940–1996*, (GC Books Ltd, 1997.)

There were similar problems caused by adverse weather conditions affecting operations in Lough Foyle and the U-boats stored there. The following accounts describe the fate of *U-975* and *U-3514*, towed out from Lisahally on 9 February 1946 in the company of frigates HMS *Loch Arkaig* and HMS *Loch Shin* together with the tug *Prosperous*:

By dawn on Sunday the 10th, it was evident that the group would not reach position XX before dark on Sunday evening. I did not want to deal with *U-975* in the weather conditions prevailing and on receipt of NOIC message timed at 101125 I decided to cast off the tow at 1500. My intention was to attack *U-975* with the 4 inch gun, followed by Shark, followed by Squid. The gun action started at 1537. Own ship was rolling and pitching badly even on the most favourable courses and the enemy disappeared behind the crests of the waves so frequently that it was obvious that the gun's crew were getting no value from the practice, and the U-boat looked fairly safe. After 15 rounds had been fired, I ceased fire and decided to abandon any attempt to use Shark.

The Squid attack started at 1559. I could get no Asdic contact at all. I therefore decided to attack by eye, approaching from the westward, and using the 20 foot single layer manual setting on the Squid. My attacking speed was 8 knots and the starboard mounting fired at 1608. The bombs straddled the U-boat, two falling over and one short. They exploded correctly, and when the water subsided, *U-975* was lying in an oily scum, the only visual damage being an apparent split in the casing forward, and some damage on the bandstand and conning tower. However, she slowly trimmed by the bows on an even keel and stood on her nose, and the stern disappeared below the surface at 1610.

U-3514 was the last U-boat to be destroyed in Operation Deadlight. On the morning of Tuesday 12 February 1946 HMS *Loch Arkaig* fired five 4 inch shells at the U-boat. Only one shell hit the casing forward of the conning tower. She then strafed *U-3514* with close-range weapons, but the U-boat refused to succumb. HMS *Loch Arkaig* next fired six Shark projectiles, of which two hit amidships and one struck a glancing blow to the conning tower but did not explode. The commander of HMS *Loch Arkaig* then ordered the ship to break off and prepare for another attack run using Squid missiles. Whilst the frigate was manoevring into attack position, the bows of *U-3514* began to sink. She was observed to hang almost vertically for a moment, and then slid under water. HMS *Loch Arkaig* lost contact with *U-3514* at a depth of 600 feet.

Thirty of the Operation Deadlight U-boats were allocated to the Fleet Air Arm and Coastal Command as practice targets. The 3rd Submarine Flotilla was also allowed to practise on other U-boats, although they were strikingly marked in yellow and red paint in order to distinguish them from the German targets. Seven U-boats were disposed of in this way, by the British submarine HMS *Tantivy*.

The final group of three U-boats left Loch Ryan on 28 December 1945. The following is the message despatched on that date confirming the completion of the Loch Ryan part of the exercise:

> From: Capt. S/M Loch Ryan   Date   28.12.45
> Time   1440
> Addressed to   C in C Rosyth,   F.O i/c Greenock,   Admiralty F.O. S/M.
> Operation Deadlight.   My 281107
>
> U-boats towed away today were *U-1233*, *U-680*, *U-1103*. Total number towed away – 86
> Only U-boats now remaining are the 3 chosen for retention. *U-712*, *U-953* and *U-2348*
> which will be sailed to Lisahally, weather permitting, on Sunday 30th.
>   281144Z
>   Advance copy sent D.C. and O.D.
> (Holme, 1997.)

Of the 86 U-boats destroyed from the Loch Ryan base under Operation Deadlight 18 were sunk by gunfire, 17 foundered and one was despatched by demolition charges en route to the designated scuttling area; of those which did reach the target zone 29 were sunk by gunfire, one by demolition charges, 13 by aircraft attack and 7 by submarine action.

There was a certain level of local disquiet at this perceived squandering of vital resources from a population so recently accustomed to the severe shortages imposed by wartime conditions. Furthermore, if the U-boats had to be destroyed, why could they not be dismantled either at Cairnryan – where a new port facility had been developed specifically for wartime use – or in the vicinity of Belfast? Employment could thereby be provided during the ship-breaking process in localities in sore need of engineering jobs for returning servicemen, but each of these pleas was ignored – the decision to scuttle the U-boats had been agreed.

Fifty years later various proposals emerged to raise some or all of the scuttled Operation Deadlight U-boats. The attraction was the perceived supply of 'clean' steel the wrecks could provide, and the question of war graves did not arise. Since the boats had been built from steel produced in the pre-Atomic Age they provided a ready source of uncontaminated non-radioactive metal essential for the production of instruments and monitoring equipment used for measuring or detecting radiation levels. Steel free of all background contamination is imperative for these instruments.

Advances in salvage technology and the great expense involved in making post-1945 steel 'clean', coupled with the rapidly diminishing supply of pre-1945 uncontaminated steel (from sources such as Scapa Flow or the Pacific, for instance) suggested that recovery of the Operation Deadlight U-boats might be economically viable. But no detailed salvage scheme has been either proposed or implemented, and the changing world situation probably means that the north Atlantic U-boats will remain where they were consigned in the middle of the twentieth century.

As *The Scotsman* saw it

The Scotsman in this case is *The Scotsman*, Scotland's national newspaper. During my researches I laboriously trawled through micro-fiche back copies of the local Sutherland paper *The Northern Times* (affectionately known in these parts as 'The Raggie') for a report, or even a snippet, a hint of those momentous events taking place on the very north coast of the far-north-westernmost county on the British mainland, but found nothing.

At this point I began to realise just how effective wartime press censorship had been, and how that frame of mind continued well after the outbreak of peace.

We are fortunate that copies of *The Scotsman* from 1817 onwards are available for inspection online. I am really very grateful indeed that I could examine newspaper reports of the time at leisure and from the comfort of my own monitor. And I am doubly grateful that *The Scotsman* appears to have been the one newspaper in Scotland favoured with inclusion on the circulation lists of Admiralty and other armed forces press releases covering the relevant period. It made the research process so much less arduous. But it also makes clear the continuing tentacles of news-management still gripping the news media at the time. It is obvious, even at this remove, that good news stories were preferred over hard news. The nation needed lifting.

The reports following in this chapter are extracts from archive copies of *The Scotsman*. All are clearly based on central authority press releases. But the advantage is that from this one source it is possible to piece together a continuous narrative telling the basics of all the various facets of the surrender, arrest and destruction of the U-boats and of the way in which that story inevitably impinged upon the lives of ordinary people gradually becoming accustomed again to peacetime.

Times were hard in the immediate postwar months, as they had been for the past six years, but there were opportunities for levity, as on the occasion when a captured U-boat being taken on a meet-the-people tour almost foundered because of nothing more unexpected than an ebbing tide. And the first grumblings of dissent at the perceived waste of resources were being heard. That the U-boats should be sunk in the deep Atlantic was unacceptable to those hard-pressed British nationals who so recently had to sacrifice their iron gates and railings to the war effort. What a waste of *sehr gut Kruppenstahl*, and British job opportunities.

I accept that some of the following reports and extracts are not wholly restricted to the events taking place in and around Loch Eriboll. But they do put into context the wider international scene in which Loch Eriboll played such a crucial part.

Wednesday, 9 May 1945

GERMAN FLEET

Admiralty's Orders for Surrender

'REPORT POSITIONS'

The Admiralty announce that the following orders have been issued for the surrender of the German Fleet:

All German and German-controlled warships, auxiliaries, merchant ships, and other craft at sea are being ordered to report their position in plain language to the nearest Allied wireless telegraph station, and are being given orders to proceed to such Allied ports as directed. They will remain in these ports until further directions are received.

All warships, auxiliaries, merchant ships and other craft in harbour are being ordered to remain in harbour.

U-boats at sea are being ordered to surface, to fly a black flag or pennant, and to report their position in plain language to the nearest Allied wireless telegraphy station. They will then proceed on the surface to such port as they may be directed.

All warships and merchant ships, whether in port or at sea, are being instructed to train all weapons fore and aft, breech blocks will be removed from guns, and torpedo tubes will be unloaded. In harbour all ammunition, explosives, torpedo warheads and all portable weapons will be landed.

Minesweeping vessels and salvage vessels, though similarly disarmed, will be instructed to complete with fuel if necessary, and to prepare themselves immediately for minesweeping or salvage service as directed. Instructions will be given for boom defences at ports and harbours to be kept open. Demolition charges and controlled minefields at all ports and harbours are to be rendered ineffective.

All personnel will be ordered to remain either on board their ships or in their establishments until other directions are received.

Friday, 11 May 1945

51 GERMAN SHIPS SURRENDER TO BRITISH SQUADRON
Copenhagen Harbour Scenes

After a perilous voyage through German minefields in the Skagerrak and Kattegat, British surface vessels have penetrated into the Baltic for the first time for five years, and at Copenhagen on Wednesday received the surrender of the last remnants of the German surface fleet, writes a naval observer. It was the final major war operation of Home Fleet forces.

The enemy vessels were headed by the powerful cruisers, *Prinz Eugen* and *Nurnberg*, looking pictures of dejection and misery. Only a few days ago they were shelling the Danish capital.

With them in the harbour were two large destroyers, one small destroyer, two torpedo boats, ten M class minesweepers, 13 flak ships, 19 armed trawlers, and two armed merchant ships, one of them belonging to the 'Altmark' class – a total of 51 ships.

The British warships were under the command of Captain Herbert Williams, RN, in the cruiser *Birmingham*, and the cruiser *Dido* and the destroyers *Zephyr*, *Zealous*, *Zodiac* and *Zest* completed the squadron.

As a smiling Danish port pilot took the ships down the winding channel, not a Nazi flag was to be seen. All the ships' masts were bare, and the crews were leaning over the guard rails watching glumly.

U-BOATS SURRENDERING
Two Enter Loch Eriboll

Two U-boats surrendered yesterday afternoon to the Royal Navy at Loch Eriboll, a remote sea inlet on the north coast of Sutherland, near Cape Wrath.

In Weymouth Bay yesterday morning, only a mile out from the animated sea front, the first German submarine surrendered to the British Navy.

She was the *U-249*, and had on board five officers and 43 ratings. She is believed to have been at sea 40 days. Her young-looking commander is Oberleutnant Kock [sic].

The U-boat had surfaced 50 miles south south-west of the Lizard on Wednesday, and two Plymouth sloops, *Amethyst* and *Magpie* were ordered to escort her into Weymouth Bay for the surrender.

The *U-249* first surrendered to a US Navy Liberator patrol bombing plane off the Scilly Islands. The U boat was seen to be flying a black flag as she surrendered.

When first sighted off Portland by the ships which had put out from Portland harbour, the U-boat was seen to be flying the British ensign over the German flag.

It was warm and sunny on a fairly calm sea when Commander N.J. Weir, RN, boarded the submarine, which came to anchor tied up to a drifter between her two escorts. A Polish armed guard was also put aboard the submarine.

Commander Weir went into the conning tower of the submarine and said to the Oberleutnant 'I have come on board to accept unconditional surrender of your U-boat'. The U-boat commander's reply in English was terse. 'I have to', he said. Then he signed the instrument of surrender.

Commander Weir afterwards delivered the instrument of surrender to Rear-Admiral R.J.R. Scott in his office in Portland Dockyard. The Rear-Admiral then signed it. He ordered the following signal to be made: 'The German ensign is to be hauled down at sunset tonight (Thursday), and it is not to be hoisted again'.

Saturday, 12 May 1945

SURRENDER OF THE U-BOATS

Escorted to Britain by Coastal Command

COMING IN STEADILY

RAF Coastal Command aircraft are escorting in surrendering U-boats, states the Air Ministry News Service.

A large number of U-boats have now flashed 'surrender signals', but not all the submarines are accessible to Coastal Command aircraft.

Some are in mid-Atlantic, others near the Newfoundland coast. U-boats in the north Atlantic are being escorted to Loch Eriboll, on the north-west coast of Sutherland, and those in the south Atlantic to Weymouth Bay.

Sunderland and Catalina flying boats, Wellingtons and long-range Liberators are circling the U-boats, which are fully surfaced and proceeding to surrender localities. Depth charges and guns are at the ready, to ensure that there is no treachery by the Germans.

SIGHTED OFF HEBRIDES

U-1058 was sighted by a Liberator, captained by Flight Lieutenant Meeres, of Fairfield Road, Tunbridge Wells, 120 miles from Benbecula, in the Outer Hebrides, proceeding at

10 knots. The crew were on deck. The Liberator continued to escort for just under two hours, when it was relieved by another Liberator, which continued escort duties.

S-293 [sic: should be *U-297*] was sighted, proceeding at 12 knots through heavy seas, by a Liberator on Thursday, 125 miles off the Outer Hebrides.

'About five Germans were in the conning tower' said the Liberator captain, Flight Lieutenant H.M. March. 'They didn't seem very pleased to see us.'

'I have been hunting for U-boats and protecting convoys in Ansons, Whitleys and Liberators day after day for five years, and during that time I have only had an opportunity to attack one periscope. It was very pleasing, however, to sight a U-boat surrendering after all those years on patrol.'

SEVEN NOW IN SCOTTISH LOCHS

Another U-boat entered Loch Eriboll last evening to surrender, bringing the number there to five and the total so far in British harbours to nine.

Two of yesterday's arrivals surrendered in Loch Alsh, between Skye and Cromarty.

Describing the scene at Loch Eriboll on Thursday, a naval reporter writes – 'When the first two U-boats were reported approaching the loch Captain M.J. Evans, OBE, DSC, RN, of Crawley, Sussex, Training Captain to the C-in-C, Western Approaches, and commanding officer of HMS *Philante*, peace-time pleasure cruising yacht, and now anti-submarine training vessel, went out in one of the MLs under his command to see for himself the first surrender.

As we drew alongside we could see the bearded faces of the crew and the grey-green uniforms and peaked caps of the officers. Several ratings stood fore and aft ready to catch heaving lines.

We looked for the swastika flag, but it was not flying. Only the ragged dark green surrender flag was flapping at the mast. Later one of the U-boat officers told me that his ensign had been thrown overboard. I took his remaining battle ensign as a prize for the *Philante*.

As the officer in charge of the boarding party reached the bridge the U-boat's commanding officer proffered a rather lame Nazi salute, and the U-boat surrendered.

A few seconds later the White Ensign flew from the mast of the conning tower – the Royal Navy had taken over.

Saturday, 12 May 1945

A SCOTSMAN'S LOG

Eriboll

It has taken the end of the war to bring lonely Loch Eriboll into the news. Eriboll lies in one of the most inaccessible regions of the Scottish mainland,

and the U-boat commanders who gave themselves up to the Navy there would see, if they did not appreciate, Highland scenery at its wildest.

We have heard very little of what has been going on in those remote Highland parishes during the war. But we may take it that, as in the Great War, they have been the scene of much activity. North-west Scotland abounds in good anchorages, and its very remoteness is, from the Navy's point of view, an added advantage.

Since this part of Scotland is sparsely populated, security precautions are more easily enforced than in densely inhabited areas.

In the days immediately preceding the war some of the western sea lochs were already 'mobilised'. It was a not uncommon sight for the holiday-maker, on sailing up some desolate Highland loch, to see a great oil tanker lying at anchor. The Navy was taking no risks.

Monday, 14 May 1945

U-BOAT SURRENDER

14 Now at British Bases

MOST IN SCOTTISH LOCHS

U-boats at British bases now number 14. Some are being taken to assembly points after having been escorted to the bases, chiefly Loch Eriboll and Lochalsh.

After a nine weeks patrol almost continuously submerged and using her snorkel, the crew of the U-boat *U-826* saw daylight again this week-end, when the submarine surrendered to the Royal Navy at Loch Eriboll.

Despite her long patrol, the U-boat was well stocked with food.

Standing on the bridge of the U-boat as it proceeded in the wake of a trawl-er to anchor farther down the loch under armed guard, her commander commented: 'When I was at school we used to sing a Scottish song about "My Heart's in the Highlands, my heart is not here" '– and he indicated the surrounding hills with a humorous shake of the head.

The first U-boat to surrender to the US – the *U-858* – will formally do so today (Monday) at the mouth of Delaware Bay, 200 miles south of New York, New York radio reported last night.

Tuesday, 15 May 1945

34 U-BOATS HAVE SURRENDERED
Between 50 and 70 Were at Sea When War Ended

Admiral Sir Max K. Horton, C-in-C Western Approaches, who at Londonderry last night received the surrender of eight U-boats which arrived from Loch Eriboll, told a reporter that from certain information the number of U-boats at sea at the signing of Germany's capitulation was between 50 and 70.

Of them, some 34 had been accounted for on both sides of the Atlantic, most of them on this side. It was likely that some might not have received the surrender instructions.

Two more U-boats surrendered last night, at Loch Eriboll, bringing the total held in the United Kingdom to 17.

The eight U-boats which reached Londonderry were delayed by a gale. They were manned by skeleton German crews under the orders of British naval personnel. They were escorted up Lough Foyle by the ships HMS *Hesperus*, the frigates HMCS *Thetford Mines*, and the US destroyer *Paine*. The U-boats all flew the White Ensign. One flew from the barrel of a 40 mm gun trained skyward.

As the vessels drew alongside the jetty they were watched by the Prime Minister of Northern Ireland, Sir Basil Brooke, and high ranking officers of the Allied services. Admiral Horton, accompanied by Sir Basil Brooke, boarded one of the submarines. Afterwards he interviewed the commanding officers of the U-boats.

A naval officer who travelled from Scotland in one of the submarines said that when he told German officers of the Belsen atrocities they said 'such things were propaganda' and would not believe they had happened.

Seven of the U-boats were of 500 tons and one of 750 tons. In some cases the guns had been removed from their mountings. The arrivals were 'a token party'.

U-boats are still surrendering in the Atlantic, but in the meantime the escorting of convoys is not being relaxed. About 100 have been found in their French Atlantic lairs and others in Norway.

COASTAL COMMAND ESCORT

RAF Coastal Command carried out its first 'victory patrols' yesterday, when three aircraft escorted the eight surrendered submarines. A Sunderland flying-boat, a Leigh light Wellington, and a long-range Liberator were detailed for the job.

At 6 a.m., a grey morning with patches of fog and a choppy sea, the aircraft made contact with the naval force at the rendezvous. Then from North Scotland to the Northern Ireland coast the three aircraft continually circled the convoy.

The 'clicks' in the aircraft, which have so many times before meant 'bombs away', now meant that more photographs had been taken. Five miles from the Northern Ireland coast the aircraft finished their patrol, signalling farewell to the convoy, which then steamed into Londonderry.

A squadron based in Northern Ireland provided the Liberator, which was captained by W.O. W.A. Ryder, of Swinton, Manchester; the Leigh light Wellington from a squadron operating from the Hebrides was captained by an Australian; the Sunderland was from Northern Ireland and captained by Flight Lieutenant P.W.G. Burgess, Ramsgate.

SURRENDER AT DUNDEE

Crew Did Not Know Till Sunday that War was Over

A crowd, numbering about 1,000, assembled at King George Wharf, at Dundee Harbour yesterday, to witness the arrival of a U-boat which had come into the Tay to surrender. The vessel, *U-2326*, of 250 tons, and one of the latest type, was escorted up river by a motor launch and a naval fishing smack. When she was berthed at the wharf a Royal Navy chief petty officer boarded her, ripped off the German naval flag, and hoisted the White Ensign. While the German flag was being taken down, the German officers stood at the salute on the conning tower.

First ashore were two young officers, then two naval ratings, the second of whom clapped his hands as he stepped onto the quay. On shore, the crew of fifteen, wearing a greyish green uniform, blue forage caps and dungarees, lined up to be searched. They were unshaven, and badly needed a haircut.

A Dutch naval rating was interpreter, and he informed the senior officer that the submarine would be inspected for explosives. The U-boat was then inspected, and small arms, including tommy-guns, ammunition and a scuttling charge, were brought ashore. The crew were left standing on the quay for more than an hour, during which time they were particularly interested in a Barracuda dive-bomber, and two Mosquito fighter-bombers which flew low over the harbour.

The German commander and engineer officer, who had accompanied the search party, then appeared on the conning tower carrying maps and charts. Shortly afterwards the German commander, accompanied by a senior officer, came ashore and left for interrogation. The crew were then dismissed by the third in command, who spoke in German. They went aboard the U-boat under escort.

It was learned that there were still six days provisions aboard the submarine. The crew did not know till Sunday that Germany had surrendered, as their wireless was out of order. The U-boat will remain in the Tay for a few days before joining the rest of the surrendered pack at an assembly point.

Wednesday, 16 May 1945

U-BOAT TIME LIMIT PREDICTED
Destruction for Those Not Surrendering
US SPOKESMAN'S VIEW

At least 38 U-boats had surrendered up to last night – 20 of them in British ports. Of the others which have surrendered, two are at Gibraltar, two are in Canadian ports, one is in Kiel and the remainder are either in United States hands or making for Allied ports.

Two more are expected to arrive today at Londonderry, where during the next month groups of U-boats will be brought to the naval base. One which is expected to berth at Liverpool today will later be open to inspection by the public.

One of the eight which surrendered at Londonderry on Monday had been at sea for 90 days.

A US Navy spokesman expressed the belief in Washington yesterday that there are still some 10 to 20 U-boats in Western Atlantic waters which have not yet indicated their intention to surrender, although he thought they would do so shortly.

Seven had been accounted for, he said: one had arrived at Lewes, Delaware, and four more were under naval escort and expected in ports soon.

All submarines reporting west of a line running north and south through the Azores were instructed to report to North American ports. Those east of the line were being sent to British ports.

The spokesman predicted that a date and time would be set for the remaining submarines to surrender. Those failing to do so would be hunted down and destroyed.

'UNSUITABLE FOR FAR EAST'

A British naval officer said yesterday that he did not believe that the U-boats would be of much use for the war in the Far East, as in tropical climate the conditions for the crews would be unbearable compared with those in British submarines of the same size.

The U-boats could not be compared favourably with British submarines, he added. Conditions on board were very uncomfortable, because the strengthening of the hull to withstand the strain of rough Atlantic conditions had reduced whatever spare room there was.

Thursday, 17 May 1945

ANOTHER U-BOAT SURRENDERS IN WEYMOUTH BAY

Another German submarine, the *U-176*, surrendered in Weymouth Bay yesterday. She was escorted by two corvettes and a flying boat, and a Liberator was circling round her when she came to anchor.

Two more German submarines, *U-825* and *U-956*, which had previously surrendered at Loch Eriboll, arrived at Londonderry naval base yesterday escorted by the frigate *Bligh*. The two U-boats are of the 500 ton class.

There are now 12 U-boats at Londonderry naval base.

A U-boat, captured while bringing supplies from Japan to Germany, is due to reach Merseyside today. The submarine is the *U-532*, one of the biggest of its type.

Wednesday, 23 May 1945

MISHAP TO 'EXHIBITION' U-BOAT AT LONDON

The German submarine *U-776*, the first U-boat to surrender at Weymouth, was taken to London yesterday for public exhibition at Westminster Pier, where she tied up about midday. In the evening, with the falling tide, the hawsers connecting her with the bank broke, and the U-boat, after settling over at an acute angle, drifted some yards before the Port of London authority men made her secure. Her British crew were unharmed and went ashore by an improvised landing bay.

As the *U-776* went up-river on the way to her berth in the forenoon sirens of merchant ships lying in the Pool hooted derisively. The vessel, which is 220 feet long, belongs to the class used to attack Atlantic convoys. She had been commissioned a year, and had had one patrol of about 50 days when she surrendered.

Four more German U-boats arrived at Londonderry yesterday, bringing the total number of submarines now there to twenty. Four other U-boats are expected at Londonderry this morning.

Monday, 11 June 1945

SURRENDERED U-BOATS AT LOCH RYAN

Surrendered U-boats have continued to reach Lochryan, Wigtownshire, and on Sunday there were 52 submarines lying in the loch. Forty of them are ocean-going craft of 750 tons, and the remainder are of the 250 ton coastal type.

None of the vessels is open to the public meantime.

Tuesday, 19 June 1945

MORE U-BOATS ARRIVE AT LERWICK

Two British-manned U-boats flying the White Ensign arrived at Lerwick yesterday afternoon from Norway, where they had surrendered.

They were escorted by a British sloop, and were diverted to Lerwick because of a gale warning.

Friday, 29 June 1945

OVER 60 U-BOATS NOW AT LOCH RYAN

More surrendered U-boats arrived at Loch Ryan, Wigtownshire, yesterday and over 60 are now moored in groups about a mile from the shore. One of the ocean-going type will be open to the public tomorrow and Monday.

Thursday, 15 November 1945

FATE OF GERMAN FLEET
Over 100 U-boats to be Scuttled
ATLANTIC GRAVEYARD
By Commander Kenneth Edwards, RN, *Daily Telegraph* and *Scotsman* Naval Correspondent

Plans are almost complete, I understand, for the greatest wholesale scuttling of war vessels since the German Fleet went down at Scapa

Flow after the 1914–18 war – sunk by the German crews who had been left aboard.

These plans, which are likely to be fulfilled within the next two or three weeks, concern the final disposal of the remains of Germany's U-boat fleet.

All the U-boats scuttled at Flensburg, Eckernfoerde, Kiel, and other German naval ports have been de stroyed by detonating explosive charges fixed by divers.

There remain more than 100 U-boats which have been collected at Loch Ryan, on the west cost of Scotland, and at Lisahally, in Northern Ireland. They are to be towed into the Atlantic and sunk outside the 300 fathom line.

The number involved makes this a complicated operation which cannot be completed in one day. When it is completed, there will remain of Germany's great U-boat fleet only 18 units. Britain, France and Russia are each to retain six for experimental purposes. Each country will retain at least two of the 1600 ton 'Type 21' submarines which were coming into service at the end of the war.

These, capable of 16 knots submerged, were tested to a depth of 900 feet, and could spend more than five months at sea without surfacing.

With the U-boat fleet destroyed, there will remain of the German Navy only the surface warships which have been collected at Wilhelmshaven. They are to be shared among some of the Allies.

Saturday, 24 November 1945

PROPOSAL TO SCUTTLE 100 U-BOATS
Galloway MP's Protest

Mr John McKie, MP for Galloway, has had several consultations with Admiralty officials in London this week in an attempt to secure the abandonment of the proposal to scuttle 100 U-boats at present in Loch Ryan.

From his house at Auchencairn, Kirkcudbrightshire, Mr McKie has sent a telegram to Mr A.V. Alexander, First Lord of the Admiralty, protest-ing strongly against the proposal. Local feeling, he says, is unanimously against it, in view of the terrible loss of material involved, and the fact that plenty of local labour is available to assist in scrapping the vessels.

Reports are current in Stranraer that the scuttling of the U-boats will commence at the beginning of next week.

Tuesday, 27 November 1945

A SCOTSMAN'S LOG
Fate of the U-boats

One can easily sympathise with the people who object to the 100-odd German U-boats at Loch Ryan being taken out to sea and sent to the bottom. It may be that to reduce a U-boat to scrap is a difficult and uneconomic business; nevertheless, to scuttle these repulsive vessels seems uncommonly like wasteful conduct, even though it may avoid squabbling among the United Nations.

Ever since we parted with our garden railings we have regarded anything constructed of metal parts as being of priceless value. The Government have dinned into our ears the monstrous folly of waste in any shape and form to the extent that now we treasure even little scraps of paper. It is going to be a little difficult to get used to the concept of redundancy again.

Tuesday, 27 November 1945

MORE U-BOATS SAIL FOR SCUTTLING

More U-boats left Loch Ryan yesterday, bringing the number that have gone out up to a dozen. It is expected that actual scuttling operations will begin today. It is unofficially reported that 24 submarines will be scuttled, but that Britain, America, Russia and France will each retain six.

Provost McDowell, Stranraer, has not received any indication of the Admiralty's attitude to his protest against the scuttlings.

Wednesday, 23 January 1946

U-BOATS' LAST VOYAGE
Graveyard in the Atlantic

From Our Own Correspondent
Lamlash, Arran, November 30

Despite heavy seas, variable wind, ominous gale warnings for many parts of the British coastal waters, and trouble caused by snapping tow ropes, the long-term task of sinking captured German U-boats in an ignominious Atlantic graveyard progresses smoothly, though at the time of writing (this dispatch has been delayed at the request of the Admiralty) there is talk of postponing the remainder of the operation until the more congenial months of spring.

In company with British, Colonial, and foreign Press representatives I travelled to Stranraer on Tuesday of this week. I was a member of the third Press party to join the slow awkward processions which lumbered heavily from the wartime emergency port at Loch Ryan to the north Atlantic grave-yard which is sited, with ironic appro-priateness, only a few miles from the spot where the Donaldson-Atlantic liner *Athenia* was torpedoed with heavy loss of life a few hours after the declaration of war. We were told quite bluntly that the final ceremonies could not have the sensation or colour attaching to the mass scuttling of the German fleet at Scapa in June 1919. Possibly they hadn't.

As I did not reach the official sink-ing area I do not know. But I do know that the crowded hours aboard the 14-year-old sloop HMS *Fowey* (Commanding Officer Lieutenant D. O'Sullivan, MBE, RN) contained quite enough excitement, thrill, and drama to satisfy the normal person.

Our special charge was a U-boat of 500 tons, built at an estimated cost of half-a-million-pounds, and while she waddled behind us on a short stay of only 250 feet she looked as ungainly and clumsy as did the rubber horses which bobbed about in peace-time swimming pools. There was a mo-ment's consternation when *U-298* broke away, but she was quickly brought under control again and, with a steadily lengthening tow rope, she

took on an unsuspected grace and ease of movement.

During the night the wind freshened, the gentle swell became rough and broken, and it was no surprise over the breakfast table to hear that in the early hours of the morning the U-boat attached to one of the Admiralty tugs had disappeared. It was learned that she had flooded and foundered, and that her tow rope had been slipped.

Until the late afternoon of Wednesday matters proceeded uneventfully with our charge riding the sea beautifully and evidently prepared to be towed to Sandy Hook if need be. Then things began to happen.

'TOW HAS PARTED'

At fourteen minutes past four after-noon tea was interrupted by the lacon-ic message: '*Cubitt*'s tow has parted.' We rushed to the bridge and saw our companion U-boat rocking gently on the waves with *Cubitt* standing nearby, *Onslow* rapidly closing in, and *Southdown* and *Fowey* veering to starboard to keep out of the way and watch developments. We were told that *Onslow* intended to sink the U-boat by gunfire, and with true naval courtesy binoculars were produced to aid our grandstand view. At that time we were well beyond Inishtrahull, about 20 miles north west of Malin Head, on the Irish coast, and had still to go about 8 miles on our 186 mile journey to the point where *U-298* was scheduled for demolition by Fleet Air Arm planes.

But a message handed to Lt O'Sullivan altered all that. At 4.28 the following signal was sent by him to the Commanding Officer: 'I have one sick officer, suspected appendicitis. Temp 104.8. Pulse 102. General condition distressed.'

The Navy does not take long to make its mind up. Five minutes later the reply came: 'Slip your tow when *Cubitt* can see your submarine, and proceed to Campbeltown with all dispatch.' *Cubitt* bore down upon us, *U-298* was released, and by twenty minutes past five *Fowey* had turned in her tracks and was racing full speed for Campbeltown.

Yet we had time to see two of the doomed flotilla meet a deserved fate. In gathering darkness, under difficult conditions of visibility, *Onslow* opened fire with 4.7 inch guns on *Cubitt*'s U-boat. The third and fourth shots were direct hits and there were some near misses until the thirteenth (on my count) crashed into the conning tower where one of the prepared TNT charges was located. There was a loud explosion, a brilliant reddish flash, and that was the end of number one.

Our U-boat still had to be disposed of, and we were lucky to see this second 'kill'. With the beat of our engines gradually increasing and the wash at the stern steadily becoming whiter and wider, we watched the brilliant searchlights of *Onslow* and *Cubitt* dancing and playing on the narrow black pencil lying in the water. It was now almost pitch black. The range was decreased, in turn both vessels opened fire, and when the conning tower was neatly hit we presumed that *U-298* had plunged beneath the surface. This was later confirmed.

The desire of the Department of Agriculture and Fisheries was that the entire fleet of sentenced U-boats should be sunk in not less than 500 fathoms of water in order that oil pollution of spawn beds should be prevented. We saw their wish ignored and part of a carefully devised scheme abandoned (the two submarines now lie in 42 fathoms) in order that a chance of life should be given to a humble 19-year-old midshipman. In an emergency the Navy stands on no ceremony.

We were into Campbeltown by 3.30 a.m. Before we left at midday we learned that the young midshipman, who had been certified as suffering from an unusual form of pleurisy, was out of danger.

Wednesday, 23 January 1946

THREE POWERS SHARING GERMAN FLEET
Operable Surface Units and 30 U-Boats
ALL OTHERS SUNK
Britain Offers France Some of the Warships

A British–Soviet–US communiqué issued last night disclosed that it was decided at the Berlin Conference that operable surface units of the German Fleet, including units which could be made operable within a specified time, together with 30 U-boats, should be divided equally between the three Powers, and that the remainder of the German Fleet should be destroyed.

A Tripartite Naval Commission was accordingly appointed to make recommendations to implement this decision, and it has recently reported to the Governments of the three Powers.

Its report is now under consideration by these Governments, but its recommendation on the allocation of the main units has been accepted, and their division between the three Powers is now being made. Surplus U-boats in U.K. ports have been sunk in accordance with this agreement.

The Foreign Office stated last night:

As announced today, a third of the operable surface units and ten submarines of the German Fleet have been allocated to the United Kingdom on the recommendation of the Tripartite Naval Commission.

His Majesty's Government have offered to transfer a number of these German warships to the French Govern-

ment, and the discussions on French requirements are now taking place between the naval experts of the two Governments.

Under the terms of the Potsdam Agreement, held in July last year, it was stated in Paragraph V:

The conference agreed in principle upon arrangements for the use and disposal of the surrendered German Fleet and merchant ships. It was decided that the three Governments should appoint experts to work out together detailed plans to give effect to the agreed principles.

The remnants of the German Fleet left Wilhelmshaven and other North German ports to be handed over under the terms of the Potsdam Agreement.

Early this month the last of the 110 U-boats were sunk by the Royal Navy in the area north-west of Bloody Foreland (Donegal). Only 30 U-boats were then left in existence, and Britain, the United States, and Russia were each allocated ten for experimental purposes.

Monday, 4 February 1946

EX-GERMAN SHIPS

France to Get Share of Britain's Allocation

FIVE DESTROYERS

Five destroyers – two of the Narvik class, two others the Maas, and one Elbing – and two torpedo boats which were part of Britain's allocation of the German Fleet, have been transferred to the French Government, stated the Foreign Office yesterday. A second Elbing destroyer will be handed over shortly.

The British Government has also lent to the French two ex-German submarines.

The destroyers and torpedo boats, which will be transferred from the British to the French Government at a ceremony at Cherbourg today, represent more than half the ships of these classes allocated to the United Kingdom by the Tripartite Naval Commission. The ships, most of them of very modern design, are being transferred outright, and will become French property.

The two U-boats will be lent for two years, after which they will revert to Britain.

Discussions on further classes of ships to be transferred from our allocation are continuing.

The Confusion Surrounding the Norwegian Royal Yacht

Philante *was the fastest, most powerful and luxurious diesel-powered pre-war private yacht. In 1937 she was commissioned by Tommy (Thomas Octave Murdoch; later Sir T.O.M.) Sopwith for his own enjoyment and as a floating base from which to pursue his passion for J class and 12 metre ocean yacht racing. She is seen here in her original conformation shortly after completion by Camper and Nicholsons. In 1939, with the worsening international situation, Sopwith sold the vessel to the Admiralty (Author's collection)*

As HMS Philante *she eventually became the command yacht of the Commander in Chief of Western Approaches, from which all of the U-boat surrenders in northern waters were coordinated.* Philante *was present in Loch Eriboll throughout the period in question, and supervised the surrender of many of the U-boats. Here she is seen bringing in two surrendered U-boats, pictured from a naval aircraft (Imperial War Museum)*

Sopwith bought back Philante *after her war service, but in the meantime had purchased a replacement private vessel.* Philante *was purchased from him by the Association of Norwegian Ship Owners in 1947 with the help of a public appeal, and presented to King Haakon VII as recognition of his 75th birthday and his steadfast resistance to the German occupation. A promise to the new king, made in 1905, was thereby fulfilled. In July 1948 she was commissioned as the Norwegian Royal Yacht KS* Norge, *a duty she carries out to this day (Author's collection)*

This photograph, taken from the Canadian frigate HMCS Nene, *perhaps started the false suggestion that the Norwegian Royal Yacht accompanied the group of 15 U-boats arrested in Norwegian waters on 17 May 1945. There was no Royal Yacht in 1945, but the imposing vessel seen here (middle of three) beyond the surrendering U-boat approaching* Nene *was at the time mistakenly thought to have been so. The vessel was actually the former Norwegian cruise liner* Stella Polaris *which had been commandeered on the fall of Norway in 1940 and had been used as a rest and recreation ship for U-boat crews (Dan DeLong/Nene collection)*

Above: Stella Polaris *is seen here in the pre-war years during her initial incarnation as a luxury cruise liner (Author's collection)*

…and right in full camouflage markings in wartime use by the Kriegsmarine as a recreation vessel for U-boat crews. An unidentified U-boat is moored alongside (Author's collection)

Above: Among the surface ships accompanying the fifteen U-boats arrested in Norwegian waters on the 17 May 1945, was this fine vessel, Aviso Grille. *She had been built in the immediate pre-war years as a private launch for Adolf Hitler, who was a notoriously bad sailor prone to sea-sickness, and he seldom used her. She eventually became the HQ vessel for FdU Noordmeer, Reinhard (Teddy) Suhren (Commander in Chief, German Arctic and Barents Sea areas), which is how she came to be accompanying the flotilla of U-boats on 17 May.* Aviso Grille *has also been suggested as a candidate for the spurious Norwegian Royal Yacht but her overall size – half that of the stronger contender – mitigates against this (Author's collection)*

Left: A photograph of Aviso Grille *taken from HMCS* Nene *at the time of the mass arrest shows her fine lines. The caption to this photograph refers also to her possibly being the former Norwegian Royal Yacht, a theory now disproved (Dan DeLong/Nene collection)*

130

POSTSCRIPT

So what remains of the surrender of the German submarine fleet in Loch Eriboll? What clues are to be found in the remote far north of Sutherland which might point to the momentous events that took place there sixty-five years ago? The answer to both questions is 'nothing'.

The 21st and 9th Escort Group frigates that accepted the surrendering U-boats left as soon as their initial task was completed. There was neither opportunity nor intention to establish semi-permanent structures which would accommodate either the British vessels or their German charges. No moorings or shore structures were built – surrendered U-boats were self-anchored or moored either to each other or to their escort vessels out in the loch. Mooring captured vessels to lochside installations would invite notions of escape from their incarcerated crews, and this was, of course, to be avoided. Eriboll was always planned as an isolated temporary holding station away from strategic installations and vital sea supply routes.

After the departure of the 21st Escort Group for the west coast and Londonderry the only naval presence in and around Loch Eriboll was a very few armed naval trawlers. They remained until June 1945, by which time the transfer of surrendered U-boats in Norway and the Baltic to the UK via the Northern Isles was complete. Norway was relieved and reoccupied by British and Norwegian forces by the third week in May; those surrendered U-boats still capable of sailing under their own power were escorted from Wilhelmshaven and the Baltic by the third week in June, travelling via Scapa Flow and/or Lerwick. Approximately 230 U-boats, including some new vessels waiting commissioning, were scuttled in the Baltic by determined commanding officers in a defiant act reminiscent of the fleet scuttling following the First World War in Scapa Flow, between 1 and 8 May 1945. Most were eventually scrapped and/or demolished by the use of explosives, a very few were raised and taken as war prizes, principally by the Soviet navy.

Loch Ryan was selected as the principal storage for the surrendered U-boats largely because of the war-time port facilities existing there. Its proximity to the national railway system, by which the crews could be dispersed to interrogation and imprisonment, was also a determining factor. Loch Alsh also was conveniently placed for the national rail network and some U-boat ratings were disembarked there for transport into captivity. The nearest railway access to Loch Eriboll was, and remains, over 50 miles away, at Lairg. There was a prisoner-of-war camp at Watten, 80 miles away to the east near Thurso, but the delivery of arrested personnel there from Loch Eriboll would present numerous opportunities for escape. And Camp 165 at Watten would not be entirely appropriate for both officers and ratings in all cases.

Loch Eriboll remains now almost as it has always been from the dawn of time.

There is a stone pier at Port-na-con on the western side of the loch. That pier was constructed in the nineteenth century before the road that is now the A.838 to Tongue was built. In those days the Heilam ferry ran from Port-na-con across Loch Eriboll to Ard Neackie, where there was an inn. The Port-na-con pier did have a timber extension, now demolished, at which sailors disembarked to visit the one shoreside establishment that gave them some connection with the real world and their families far away.

That facility was the post office and general store at Laid, which attracted long lines of servicemen snaking their way between Port-na-con and Laid. Pay could be deposited at the post office, and the very few basic items available in wartime could be purchased, or often bartered. It is still possible, after all this time, to discern the narrow track leading from the landing place to Laid, wending its way on the northerly side of the small hill between the loch and the A.838 road just north of the hamlet of Laid.

But that is not the sole tangible reminder of the wartime excitements in this isolated, serene, beautiful location. High on the hillside overlooking Port-na-con the names of several warships of the Royal Navy are commemorated, the best-known of which must surely be the mighty *Hood*.

HMS *Hood* was the largest warship in the world when commissioned in 1920, a symbol of Imperial might throughout the inter-war years. She was ordered on 7 April 1916, her keel being laid on 1 September of that year. She was launched on 22 August 1918 and completed on 15 May 1920. At launch she had a displacement of 42,100 tons and a speed of 31 knots, though after modification these figures would be amended to 49,140 tons and 28 knots respectively. Although classified as a battle-cruiser, *Hood* was in truth a fast battleship, an improved version of the *Queen Elizabeth*. *Hood*'s main armament consisted of eight 15 inch guns with a secondary armament of twelve 5.5 inch guns. By 1941 six 21 inch torpedo tubes were also fitted.

Her career in the inter-war years took her on a world cruise with fellow battle-cruiser HMS *Repulse* in 1923–24 to the Far East, the Pacific and the United States. She served with the Home and Atlantic Fleets until 1936, when she was transferred to the Mediterranean. On the outbreak of the Second World War *Hood* was based in Scapa Flow, again with the Home Fleet. In June 1940 she was allocated to force H, the squadron established under Admiral James Somerville to assume French duties in the western Mediterranean.

Hood returned to the Home Fleet thereafter and on 19 May 1941 she sailed with the brand new battleship HMS *Prince of Wales* to intercept the German battleship *Bismarck*, which was attempting to break out into the north Atlantic. *Bismarck* and her compatriot the heavy cruiser *Prinz Eugen* were shadowed on radar by HMS *Norfolk* and HMS *Suffolk*, which reported their position to Admiral Holland in HMS *Hood*.

In the Denmark Strait between Greenland and Iceland on the morning of 24 May 1941 Holland ordered his ships to close range and shortly before 0600 both sides opened fire. *Bismarck*'s fifth salvo hit *Hood* amidships, penetrating the secondary armament magazine. The detonation spread to the main magazine resulting in a catastrophic explosion which tore the ship in half. Only three members of the crew of 1,421 survived.

Three days later, crippled by attacks from Fleet Air Arm aircraft, *Bismarck* was engaged by battleships HMS *King George V* and HMS *Rodney* before being sunk by torpedoes. Churchill's avowed demand that the loss of HMS *Hood* should be avenged had been satisfied.

In July 2001 the wreck site of HMS *Hood* was located 3,000 metres deep in the Denmark Strait.

HMS *Hood* is commemorated in a simple memorial on the western flank of Loch Eriboll at (approximately) map reference NC42607. The name is picked out in large stones in a clearing in the hillside, along with others commemorating HMS *Valiant*, HMS *Swift*, HMS *Whirlwind*, HMS *Sutherland* and HMS *H.43*, the sole submarine represented. The stones are looked after and periodically repainted by children from the Durness Primary School and the ground is also cleared of bracken. The memorial site is visible from the A.838 road passing southwards along the eastern side of Loch Eriboll, from above the distinctive twin-crescent promontory of Ard Neackie. It may also be glimpsed from near to the junction with the Port-na-con track on the western side. There is a memorial plaque to the tragedy of HMS *Hood* in the tiny Eriboll church, which was unveiled in May 1997.

Despite the firm intentions of the Allied governments to permanently destroy the U-boat fleet, several examples did survive the war and are available as public exhibits to this day.

U-505 (Type IXC) was launched in May 1941 from the Deutsche Werft AG (Hamburg) yard (Job No. 295) and commissioned on 26 August 1941. The boat completed ten patrols in Atlantic and Caribbean waters and sank eight vessels totalling 45,000 tons. One commander suffered a burst appendix; that patrol had to be curtailed and the vessel returned to base. The replacement commander committed suicide during a depth-charge attack. In a previous air attack on the vessel three crew members were killed.

In June 1944 *U-505* was bombed and depth-charged to the surface by aircraft of the US VC-8 squadron north-west of Dakar, West Africa. The commander and 59 crew abandoned ship under heavy gunfire and were taken prisoner, and one crew member was killed. A boarding party kept the vessel afloat and it was towed surreptitiously to Bermuda by the US Navy. The capture was kept secret and *U-505* became the USS Nemo in 1944. Ten years later *U-505* was donated to the Chicago Science Museum and put on public display, where it remains. For further details see www.msichicago.org

U-534 (Type IXC/40) was launched in September 1942 from the Deutsche Werft AG (Hamburg) yard (Job No. 352) and commissioned on 23 December 1942. The boat completed two patrols in the north Atlantic without inflicting damage or loss to Allied shipping. In August 1944 *U-534* was attacked by Wellington NB798 of 172 Squadron RAF, which it shot down in return fire. The pilot was awarded a posthumous George Cross.

On 5 May 1945 *U-534* was bombed by Liberator KH347 of 86 Squadron RAF 13 miles north-east of Arnholt, Denmark and sank with the loss of three crew. Forty-nine other crew members were rescued.

In 1993 *U-534* was raised in the Kattegat, Denmark and almost ended up as scrap, but was saved after the intervention of Danish publisher and businessman Karsten Ree and eventually taken over by the Warship Preservation Trust. In 1996 she was transferred to England and is currently on public display at Birkenhead, Merseyside.

For further details see www.web.ukonline.co.uk/gaz/U.534.html and/or www.uboatstory. co.uk

U-995 (Type VIIC/41) was launched in July 1943 from the Blohm und Voss (Hamburg) yard (Job No. 195) and commissioned on 16 September 1943. The boat completed nine war patrols in the Arctic and sank or damaged five Allied vessels totalling 22,000 tons. In late December 1944 *U-995* was almost lost to a circle-running torpedo and returned to base in a damaged state after rescuing two Soviet sailors off the Kola coast. It seems that damage inflicted by bombing action during construction made this vessel susceptible to weakness.

U-995 was surrendered in May 1945 in Trondheim, Norway having recently been decommissioned as unseaworthy. It was taken over by the Royal Navy and allocated to Norway as war booty in October 1948. On 6 December 1952 the vessel was recommissioned as the RNorN Kaura for use as a training boat. It was decommissioned for a second time on 15 December 1962 and thereafter presented to the Germany Naval Museum. It became a static exhibit and memorial at Loboe/Kielfjorde in October 1971.

For further details see www.warmuseums.nl/gal/061.htm

U-2540 (Type XXI) was launched in January 1945 at the Blohm und Voss (Hamburg) yard (Job No. 2540) and commissioned on 24 February 1945. The boat was assigned to the 31st Training Flotilla but took no part in aggressive patrols and no enemy vessels were damaged or sunk.

U-2540 was scuttled on 4 May 1945 near the Flensburg lighthouse following a cannon and rocket attack the previous day by Typhoon fighter-bombers of the 2nd TAF, RAF, in the Great Belt. The boat was raised in 1957 and recommissioned into the Federal German Navy on 1 September 1960 as the research vessel Wilhelm Bauer (Y-880). *U-2540* was transferred to the German Maritime Museum at Bremerhaven in 1984, where she remains on display and open for public inspection.

For further details see www.dsm.museum/e3ubor.htm

U-2505/ U-3004/ U-3506 are all Type XXI boats stranded in the Vulkanhafen Elbe II bunker by heavy air attacks on Hamburg at the start of May 1945. All three vessels were trapped beneath collapsed roofs or by other severe damage, and with the passage of time became forgotten as the area around the buildings in which they are buried was developed as part of the Freeport of Hamburg.

The three damaged but largely preserved vessels were rediscovered in 1985. They remain where they were entombed in 1945, although the void in which they lie has been filled with gravel to prevent unauthorised access. These three vessels are not available for public visits.

For further details seehttp://uboat.net/history/hamburg_elbe2.htm

U-1105 (Type VIIC/41) is the sole surviving U-boat to have avoided destruction or breaking from the thirty-three known to have been temporarily berthed in Loch Eriboll at the end of the Second World War. The boat, whilst not exactly enjoying a charmed life during its active service did nevertheless survive all attempts at its destruction in wartime, and even when in the hands of the Allies afterwards as a vessel retained for experimentation, assessment and evaluation, its 'lucky' status seems to have remained undiminished.

This is perhaps largely due to its unusual external configuration. Its synthetic rubber skin may well have protected it from detection during active service, and that experimental treatment certainly kept the vessel safe from inclusion in Operation Deadlight and consignment to the bottom of the Atlantic. Even when subjected to explosive testing at the end of its evaluation period in Allied hands, over four years after its surrender, the vessel's structural integrity could not be wholly compromised. It 'survives' today virtually whole and certainly recognisable as a later incarnation of the U-boat. As such it is visited by underwater archaeologists and leisure divers alike.

U-1105 is one of ten modified Type VIIC boats fitted by the Kriegsmarine with an external coating codenamed 'Alberich', an early stealth technology synthetic rubber process the aim of which was to afford some measure of protection from the asdic and sonar detection equipment deployed by Allied convoy protection vessels. The distinctive rubber-like outer skin earned the boat the name 'Black Panther'; her emblem of a panther bestriding the globe was prominently displayed on her conning tower and was regarded as something of a talisman by the crew.

The U-boat left its base at Markiven on 12 April 1945 for what turned out to be its only active war patrol. Over the next two weeks *U-1105* successfully evaded the counter-submarine measures of patrolling Allied destroyers and on the 27th she happened upon three British destroyers, part of the second division of the 21st Escort Group. Kommandant Oberleutnant zur See Hans-Joachim Schwarz fired two acoustic torpedoes then immediately dived in order to evade counter-attack measures. Both torpedoes struck HMS *Redmill* in the stern area, killing 32 crew members and severely disabling the vessel.

The search for *U-1105* extended over the following two days, but the U-boat successfully avoided detection even when she was unable to maintain her chosen depth of 330 feet and was obliged to rest on the bottom, silent and motionless, at 570 feet, for over 24 hours. *U-1105* remained undetected, after surfacing and continuing her patrol, until the capitulation announcement.

U-1105 surfaced to the north of the British Isles, recognised the surrender orders and headed surfaced along the prescribed route to Loch Eriboll where, ironically, she was arrested by sister frigates of the 21st Escort Group. The engagement with HMS *Redmill* was the only aggressive action in which *U-1105* was involved throughout her fighting career.

From Loch Eriboll she was eventually escorted for storage to Lisahally, Lough Foyle, Northern Ireland along with dozens of other U-boats, to await her fate. But her recent design characteristics and almost unique outer skin immediately proved of great interest to the Allies, and after redesignation as British Submarine N-16 (and exemption from Operation Deadlight), she was turned over to the United States as a prize of war and further evaluation of her then remarkable counter-surveillance capabilities.

In 1946 the boat arrived at the navy yards at Portsmouth, New Hampshire. The Naval Research Laboratory in Washington, DC, and the Massachusetts Institute of Technology's Acoustic Laboratory in Cambridge, Mass., each conducted research and evaluation experiments on the boat's rubber-tiled outer skin. The results have never been published, though it is known that the tiles were prone to lifting when the vessel was running submerged at speed.

After the completion of these tests *U-1105* was sunk, on 18 November 1948, in Chesapeake Bay, during explosives development and testing. But her instinct for survival remained, and in the summer of 1949 she was raised, this time as part of an on-going salvage technique development programme.

On 19 September, 1949 *U-1105* was once again sunk during tests of a new type of high-explosive Mk 5 250 pound depth charge suspended 30 feet below her hull. She sank in 91 feet and settled on her keel with 68 feet of water over her conning tower, though her pressure hull was cracked around almost the whole of her circumference. But there was virtually no debris field, and therefore little to show of her presence other than the slumbering profile.

Errors in recording her precise latitude and longitude coordinates meant that her position gradually faded from memory and she became effectively 'lost'. Only on 29 June 1985 was she relocated, by a team of sport divers who had successfully reinterpreted the true coordinates of her position.

In November 1994 the wreck of *U-1105* was designated as Maryland's first historic shipwreck preserve, and on 8 May 1995, in partnership with the United States Navy, it was formally declared open as the first underwater shipwreck preserve in the State, off Piney Point in the Potomac River. A static exhibition, funded via the Department of Defense, is open to the public at the Piney Point Lighthouse Museum. *U-1105* remains the property of the US Navy.

The wreck of *U-1105* is apparently well-preserved and largely intact. The wooden-slatted main deck fore and aft of the conning tower is occasionally exposed by drifting silt beds. In the season April to December a blue-and-white buoy marks the hull's position at 38-08.09N x 076-33.09W. The site is managed and protected by the Maryland Historical Trust.

And there is a further vessel in use today which enjoyed a significant personal involvement with the events in Loch Eriboll in May 1945. Readers will recall that attached to but not part of the 21st Escort Group sent from Londonderry to Loch Eriboll in early May 1945 was HMS *Philante*. This vessel enjoyed a very varied and extensive history, the denouement of which is with us today.

Thomas Octave Murdoch (T.O.M.) (Tommy) Sopwith (1888–1989) was a celebrated aviation pioneer, and later a leading industrialist and international yachtsman in the inter-war years. He was knighted in 1953 for services to aviation. He was born the last of eight children, hence the name 'Octave'; all of his siblings were sisters. By November 1910 he had earned his aviation licence (issue number 31) at Brooklands. Within four days he had set the British duration record of 108 miles in three hours and twelve minutes and within a month (18 December 1910) had won the de Forest prize for the longest flight from England to continental Europe, flying from Eastchurch to Tirlemont, Belgium in three hours and forty minutes, a distance of 169 miles. And all this was accomplished within seven years of the Wright brothers' first powered and controlled manned flight at Kittyhawk.

The Sopwith Aviation Company was formed in 1912. By the end of the First World War over 17,000 military aircraft had been produced, the best-known of which would be the Pup and the Camel (the most effective fighter of the First World War), wood, wire and canvas creations epitomising the formative years of aerial combat. The company was liquidated after the First World War by the actions of an Inland Revenue displaying more avarice than intellect – perceived excess profits from the war years had to be penalised. In 1920 a new concern, named the H.G. Hawker Engineering Company Limited, was formed with Harry Hawker as chief test pilot. In 1923 designer Sidney Cam joined the company (he had been trained as a pilot by Sopwith in the war years), and he later produced the Hawker Hurricane, which became the mainstay in Britain's air defences throughout the Second World War.

By a process of mergers the company became Hawker Siddeley Aviation, which eventually emerged as British Aerospace in its final incarnation following nationalisation and compulsory merger with the rival British Aircraft Corporation in 1977.

During the 1930s Thomas Sopwith established himself as perhaps the foremost of Britain's international sportsmen and a celebrated yachtsman. He funded and organised the

America's Cup challenges, with *Endeavour* in 1934 and *Endeavour II* in 1937, though without success, acting as helmsman on both occasions.

Throughout the later 1920s and 1930s Sopwith owned several private motor launches for use during both his own leisure cruising and as base vessels for his ocean racing activities. In 1936 he ordered what was to be the largest diesel-powered and most impressive of the private motor yachts of the era, from Camper and Nicholson of Gosport. *Philante* had a beam of 38 feet, an overall length of 263 feet, a draught of 15 feet 5 inches and a displacement of 1,628 tons. The vessel was launched on 11 February 1937.

The name *Philante* came from elements of his wife's name (Phyllis) and that of his son, (Thomas Edward).

In 1939 Sopwith agreed to sell *Philante* to the British Admiralty (the vessel was neither requisitioned nor commandeered) in view of the worsening international situation. She was refitted as HMS *Philante* and armed as an Atlantic convoy escort until 1942, when she became a training ship for convoy escorts. The end of the Second World War saw her acting as the Commander-in-Chief Western Approaches' yacht and as such she carried out supervisory and co-ordinating roles at the surrender of the U-boats escorted into Loch Eriboll. The records show that she arrested at least three surrendering U-boats.

By 1946 *Philante* had been decommissioned and offered back to Tommy Sopwith by the Admiralty. He agreed to purchase her (he had, after all, been able to enjoy the vessel for just a little over two years before the outbreak of war) notwithstanding that he had by then acquired a replacement vessel (later to be known as *Philante II*), an ex-Admiralty craft of 155 tons then named *Lady Helena*.

In Norway in 1947 the press appealed to the people for funds with which to purchase a yacht to be presented to King Haakon on the occasion of his 75th birthday, as recognition of his steadfast resistance to the German occupation. Attention turned to *Philante*, just ten years old but with an extensive war service record behind her. The vessel was purchased, by means of a public appeal and the good offices of the Association of Norwegian Ship Owners, for the sum of 1.5 million Norwegian kroner, and totally refurbished.

Philante was recommissioned as KS *Norge*, the Norwegian Royal Yacht, on 9 July 1948, a duty she fulfils to this day.

In this very tangible way a connection with the momentous world events that took place in Loch Eriboll during May 1945 is maintained.

But there is no local commemoration of the 59 allied merchant ships and 14 warships, comprising over 300,000 tons of shipping, damaged or sunk by the 33 surrendered U-boats escorted into Loch Eriboll mid May 1945. More significantly, there remains no memorial to the many hundreds of brave Royal Navy and Merchant Navy seamen, of Allied and other nationalities, who perished by the direct intervention of those U-boats.

Appendix 1

21ST ESCORT GROUP VESSELS

Hull No.	Ship name	Built by	Keel laid	Launched	Commiss'ed	Decommissioned etc
79	*Byron* K.508	Bethlehem Shipyard, Hingham, Mass.	24 May 1943	14 August 1943	30 October 1943	24 November 1945 and returned to US Navy. Struck 3 January 1946, and scrapped
80	*Conn* K.509	-do-	2 June 1943	21 August 1943	31 October 1943	26 November 1945 and returned to US Navy. Struck 3 January 1946, and scrapped
86	*Deane* K.551	-do-	30 June 1943	29 September 1943	26 November 1943	4 March 1946 and returned to US Navy. Struck 12 April 1946, and scrapped
88	*Fitzroy* K.553	-do-	24 August 1943	1 September 1943	16 October 1943	5 January 1946 and returned to US Navy. Struck 7 February 1946, and scrapped
89	*Redmill* K.554	-do-	14 July 1943	2 October 1943	30 November 1943	5 January 1946 and returned to US Navy 20 January 1947. Struck 7 February 1947, and scrapped

(NOTE : This vessel torpedoed 27 April 1945 in Donegal Bay by *U-1105*. 60 feet of stern section blown away and 32 crew members killed. Laid up in Lisahally thereafter. Constructive total loss. *U-1105* surrendered to HMS *Conn* (K.509) on 10 May 1945 and was escorted into Loch Eriboll).

Hull No.	Ship name	Built by	Keel laid	Launched	Commiss'ed	Decommissioned etc
96	*Rupert* K.561	-do-	25 August 1943	31 October 1943	24 December 1943	20 March 1946 and returned to US Navy. Struck 17 April 1946, and scrapped

Each of these vessels was built as part of the Buckley (TE) Class, the largest of the six classes.
154 vessels were built, of which 46 were consigned to the Royal Navy.

Appendix 2

9TH (CANADIAN) ESCORT GROUP VESSELS

Hull No.	Name	Built by	Keel laid	Launched & Comm'ed	Fate etc
Ordered 2 February 1943 Job No. J.18139 Yard No. 700	*Loch Alvie* K.428	Barclay, Curie, Dundee	31 August 1943	(L) 14 April 1944 (C) 21 August 1944	Decommissioned 1964. Sold for breaking up 20 September 1965, Singapore.
	Matane K.444	Canadian Vickers Ltd, Montreal, Quebec	23 December 1942	(L) 9 May 1943 (C) 22 October 1943	Decommissioned 2 November 1946. Sunk as a break-water at Oyster Bay, B.C., 1948
Ordered 24 January Job No. 4534 Yard No. 1110	*Nene* K.270	Smith's Dock, Middlesbrough	20 June 1942	(L) 9 December 1942 (C) 8 April 1943	Placed on Disposal List 1955. Broken by T.W.Ward Ltd 21 July 1957
	Monnow K.441	Charles Smith & Sons, Bristol	28 September 1943	(L) 4 December 1943 (C) 3 August 1944	Paid off 6 November 1945. Became Danish *Holger Dansk* 1945–59
	St Pierre K.680	Davie S & R Co. Ltd., Lauzon	30 June 1943	(L) 1 December 1943 (C) 28 August 1944	Paid off 22 November 1945 Transferred 1947 to Peru – became *Teniente Palacios*, later *Palacios*

Each of these vessels operated as a Canadian Navy (HMCS) ship and was manned by a Canadian national crew.

Appendix 3

U-BOATS APPORTIONED TO THE ALLIES

Original apportionment of captured U-boats determined by the Allies under the
Tripartite Naval Agreement of 3 November 1945

(Bold type indicates U-boats present in Loch Eriboll)

British apportionment:

Type					
	VIIC	U-712	U-953	U-1108	U-1171
	XVIIB	U-1407			
	XXI	U-2518	U-3017		
	XXIII	**U-2326**	U-2348		

United States apportionment:

Type			
	VIIC	**U-1105**	U-1023
	IXC	U-889	
	IXD	U-873	
	XB	U-234	
	XVIIB	U-1406	
	XXI	U-2502 (originally to be U-3041) U-3514 (originally to be U-3515)	
	XXVI	U-2351	U-2356

Russian apportionment:

Type				
	VIIC	U-1057	**U-1058**	U-1064 **U-1305**
	IXC	**U-1231**		
	XXI	U-2529 U-3035 U-3041 (originally to be U-2529) U-3514 (reserve boat U-3515)		
	XXIII	U-2353		

France was not allocated any U-boats under the Tripartite Agreement.
Britain decided to allocate U-2326 and U-2518 to France from its share.

Select bibliography and further reading list

Bishop, C., *Kriegsmarine U-Boats 1939–45* Spellmount Ltd, Gloucestershire, 2006

Bramson, A., *Pure Luck, The Authorised Biography of Sir Thomas Sopwith, 1888–1989*, Patrick Stephens Ltd, Somerset, 1990

Campbell, V. *Camp 165 Watten*, Whittles Publishing, Scotland, 2008 (second edition in preparation)

Durham, P., *The Führer Led But We Overtook Him*, Pentland Press, Edinburgh, 1996

Guske, H.F.K., *The War Diaries of U-764: Fact or Fiction?* Thomas Publications, Gettysburg, PA, USA, 1992

Hammerton, J.A. (Ed.), *The War Illustrated*, Vol. 9 (Issue no. 223), Amalgamated Press Ltd, London, 1946

Holme, R., *Cairnryan Military Port 1940–1996*, GC Book Publishers, Wigtown, 1997

Lansley, R., *Durness Past and Present*, Durness Local Studies Group, Durness, 1998

Lund, P. & Ludlam, H., *Atlantic Jeopardy*, Foulsham Publishing Ltd, London, 1990

Lund, P. & Ludlam, H., *Trawlers Go To War*, New English Library, England, 1975 (now Foulsham, see preceding entry)

Milner, M., *The U-Boat Hunters*, University of Toronto Press, Canada, 1994

Sharpe, P., *U-Boat Fact File*, Midland Publishing, Hinckley, 1998 (now an imprint of Ian Allan Publishing)

Tye, C.B., *The Real Cold War*, self-published, England, 1995

Articles
Williams, E., 'U-boat crews surrendered – defeated but defiant to the last' in 'The Road to VE Day' supplement, *The Scotsman*, 10 May 2005